Why Cheese and Wine Cookery?

It's natural

Not only good, but good for you.

It's economical

Cheese is the most inexpensive way to put taste-appealing protein on your table and wine converts low-priced cuts of meat into tender, tempting delights.

It's versatile

A little bit of cheddar can turn plain carrots into a mouth-watering casserole and a cup of white wine can transform ordinary chuck into fabulous Beef à la Mode.

and
It's delicious

Beef Bourguignon, Cauliflower Polonaise, Sweet and Sour Pork, Swiss Chicken Breasts, Fillets of Sole Au Gratin, Spinach Pies, Zabaglione, Fettuccine Alfredo, Swedish cucumbers, and dozens and dozens more!

Also by Carol Truax on the Ballantine Books List:

Gourmet Entertaining on a Budget

available at your local bookstore

Cheese and Wine

Good Cooking/ Good Eating

Carol Truax

BALLANTINE BOOKS · NEW YORK

To My Husband

SBN 345-24452-4-150

First Printing: August, 1975

Printed in the United States of America

BALLANTINE BOOKS
A Division of Random House, Inc.
201 East 50th Street, New York, N.Y. 10022
Simultaneously published by
Ballantine Books, Ltd., Toronto, Canada

contents

Part Three: The Partners: Wine and Cheese

before you begin

Herbs

If you can get fresh herbs, by all means do so! Use 2 to 4 times as much fresh as dried. Buy dried herbs in small amounts as they tend to lose flavor.

Reputable herb farmers know which herbs are allies and not enemies—they know what quantity to use for the herbs to complement each other. Since the experts probably know more than you do about these proportions, it is wise to purchase certain herbs already blended. *Fines herbes* is a combination of parsley, chervil, and chives, and sometimes basil and thyme. This is a most useful blend and is available almost everywhere. The same is true of *blended salad herbs*, which vary slightly from farm to farm, but usually contain tarragon, a member of the onion family, bay leaf, chervil, and parsley. There are a number of other good blends on the market, such as: *soup herbs, bouquet garni, fish herb blend, tomato herbs, and poultry seasoning.* Try them!

RECIPE CROSS REFERENCES
Names of recipes included in this book are printed in italic letters when they are mentioned in another recipe.

Canned soups are used undiluted.

part one
cheese

Once upon a time, thousands of years ago, it is said, there was a man who owned some camels. His address is not given, because he had no address. He wandered about from oasis to oasis, wherever there was food and drink for man and beast. During his travels he refreshed himself with the milk of his she-camels.

One day, so the story goes, preparing for another journey, he took his crude canteen made of a camel's stomach, filled it with milk, and hung it at his saddle bow.

Every ride on a camel is bumpy, but this was one of the bumpiest. At journey's end, the milk had been churned into nothing but thin whey and a thick lump. Making the best of it, the camel-owner tasted the lump. It was delicious! The natural rennet in the stomach-canteen had turned the milk into—cheese! And so this great food was born. It is not known how long it took for the man to discover that for turning milk into cheese, a camel ride was not necessary. But from that day to this, cheese has rated high among foods all around the world.

Cheese and Wine

The Sumerians in 4,000 B.C. recorded their stocks of cheese. As long ago as 3,000 B.C. Homer sang of cheese. The Greeks fed it to their Olympic athletes as a concentrated form of nourishment. It formed the main ration of Hebrew soldiers because it was so easy to carry. Roman men-about-town called their more toothsome girl friends "my little cheese." Today we call a weighty VIP "the big cheese."

And cheese *is* big these days, in these United States. Almost every state produces some kind of cheese. Wisconsin, Ohio, and New York are cheese country par excellence. Practically every kind of cheese produced in Europe is also produced in the United States. Moreover, we also make some native American cheeses that are second to none. American Liederkranz is one of our great contributions to the world's cheeses; and Monterey Jack is not far behind. With so many great cheeses around, no wonder the consumption of cheese in the USA has doubled in the last ten years—from 1¼ billion pounds in 1962 to 2½ billion in 1972!

More and more people are finding out what the ancient Sumerians knew. For them, cheese was the only form in which all the nutrition of the milk could be preserved; cheese today is still nutritious, portable, and appetizing, and also very long-lasting.

Cheese on your table saves money, putting nutritious protein in your diet for less. One-half pound of cheese has as much complete protein as a pound of meat, and costs much less, especially since there is absolutely no waste. You eat every ounce of cheese you pay for, which is more than you can say about a T-bone steak or a standing rib roast.

Cheese also puts flavor in your food economically. Mild or piquant, it is the most versatile of foodstuffs —equally pleasing in savories and hors d'oeuvres, as a soup or in a soup, forming or flavoring the main dish, in vegetables, as a sauce, in a sauce, with a salad, in a salad; as a course before dessert, as a course instead of dessert, as a dessert, in a dessert; as a luncheon dish, as a late-evening repast, as part of a cold collation.

There is a cheese for every taste and use, from soft to hard, from bland to pungent. The Glossary at the end of this book explains the principal kinds. Of course every kind of cheese is great for eating plain, and we'll discuss the art of cheese-eating later.

Many different cheeses lend themselves to cheese cookery equally well. A cheese dish is only as good as the cheese ingredient. Of all cheeses, the most useful in cookery is the type we call Cheddar, or American, or rat-trap. This cheese is obtainable mild, medium, sharp, and extra-sharp, according to the degree of aging. The sharper the cheese, the more pungent the flavor it lends to the dish. This cheese is for sauces, to enrich and flavor casseroles, or for melted cheese dishes. Process cheese, which melts easily, is adequate for making sauces, but real cheese is better.

Another cheese that is great for cookery is what we call Swiss. They make many cheeses in Switzerland, a country of flowery meadows where many herds graze; but in this country, Swiss cheese is the kind with the holes. American Swiss cheese is full of holes, and what's around the holes is delicious to eat and great to cook with. Our Swiss cheese is the basis of tasty fondues, delicious cheese sauces, casseroles, and soufflés.

From Italy come the pungent hard cheeses called Parmesan and Romano. The Italians grate them on pasta. They think they are best grated fresh, and past question they are right. Parmesan also perfumes French onion soup and crisply tops Chicken Tetrazzini and many other casseroles. Parmesan gives character to Veal Parmigiana. A sprinkling of grated Romano, with or without Parmesan, gives a lift to a salad.

Blue cheese, whether Roquefort, Stilton, Gorgonzola, or just American Blue, is a very piquant cheese which adds zing to salad dressings, hors d'oeuvres, and distinguished main dishes.

The soft, mild cheeses—cream, cottage, or Neufchâtel —often turn up in surprising places: cakes and cake frostings, pies, cheesecakes, *coeur à la crème,* filling a cooked pear or a peach as a dessert or a salad. Other salads also benefit from a garnish of cream cheese. Cottage cheese and cream cheese make salad dressings, sauces, and dips. And main dishes often derive their inexpensive nutriment from the cottage cheese which extends more expensive ingredients.

In short, cheese, easily stored, nutritious, inexpensive, and popular, used to be for Lent. Now it is for all the year round.

hors d'oeuvres

In summertime on the terrace, or in winter before the living room fire, what goes better with a couple of drinks than *hors d'oeuvres* made of savory cheese?

CHEESE TART

Pastry

Crumb Crust or *9-Inch Baked Pie Shell* or
6 tablespoons flour

3 tablespoons butter
3 tablespoons cold water

Filling

2 tablespoons butter
2 tablespoons flour
½ cup milk
¼ teaspoon pepper
Pinch nutmeg

2 tablespoons grated Gruyère cheese
¼ cup grated Parmesan cheese
2 eggs, separated

Preheat oven to 400°. Press the *crumb crust* into a 9-inch pie plate or use the *9-inch baked pie shell*.

Or, if you want to make the pastry crust, crumble the flour and butter together, add salt and water, and press directly into the pie pan, using your hands and knuckles. Prick with a fork, fill with dry beans, and bake at 400° for 20 minutes. Meanwhile, make the filling. Beat the egg yolks. Melt the butter, blend in the flour, and stir in the milk slowly. Season with pepper and nutmeg and cook over low heat until thickened and smooth. Stir in the Gruyère and half of the Parmesan cheese. Remove from heat and stir in the beaten egg yolks. Cool. Beat the egg whites until stiff, fold them into the cheese mixture, and pour into the pie shell. Top with remaining Parmesan cheese and bake for about 12 minutes, until lightly browned on top. *Serves 6.*

SWISS CHEESE PIE

½ pound Swiss cheese
9-inch *Unbaked Pie Shell*
3 eggs

1 cup half-and-half
½ teaspoon salt
¼ teaspoon pepper

Preheat oven to 450°. Grate the cheese and spread it over the *unbaked pie shell* in the pie plate. Beat the eggs and add the half-and-half, salt, and pepper. Mix again and pour over the cheese. Bake for 10 minutes, reduce the heat to 325°, and bake half an hour more. *Serves 6.*

CHEESE AND ONION PIE

9-inch *Unbaked Pie Shell*
1 cup chopped onion
2 tablespoons butter
2 cups shredded Swiss
    cheese

3 eggs
1 cup milk
1 teaspoon salt

Put the pie shell into a 9-inch pie plate and crimp the edges. Sauté the onion in butter until soft but not browned. Put onto the pie shell and cover with the cheese. Beat the eggs with the milk and salt. Pour over the cheese. Bake at 450° for 15 minutes; then reduce heat to 325° and bake half an hour longer. *Serves 6.*

CHEESE PUFFS

1 tablespoon butter
1 tablespoon flour
⅔ cup milk
½ pound mild or sharp
    Cheddar cheese,
    shredded

½ teaspoon salt
⅛ teaspoon pepper
2 eggs, separated
Toast rounds or squares

Melt the butter in the top of a double boiler, add the flour, and stir in the milk slowly. Add the cheese, salt, and pepper. Heat and stir until the cheese is melted. Beat the egg yolks, pour the cheese mixture into them, and mix. Beat the egg whites until stiff, and fold them into the cheese. Pile onto pieces of toast and broil, not too close to the heat, until high and browned. *Serves 8.*

CHEESE TWISTS

1 cup shredded Cheddar
    cheese
1 cup shortening
2 cups flour

½ teaspoon salt
1 tablespoon sugar
Cinnamon sugar

Combine the cheese and shortening and work them into the flour until smooth. Add salt and sugar. Form into a ball. If the dough is too stiff to handle, add a little cold water. Chill. Roll out thin and cut in strips about ½-inch wide and 4 inches long. Twist and bake the strips on a floured cookie sheet at 400° for about 8 minutes. Sprinkle with a mixture of cinnamon and sugar. *Serves 8.*

CHEESE STRAWS

¼ cup shortening
1 cup flour
¾ cup grated Cheddar
    cheese

1 egg
2 tablespoons ice water

Preheat oven to 400°. Cut the shortening into the flour with a pastry blender or two knives. Add the cheese. Beat the egg with 2 tablespoons ice water and add to the mixture. Roll out on a lightly floured board, as thin as possible—about ⅛-inch thick. Cut into narrow strips ⅓ inch by 4 inches. Bake the strips on a greased baking sheet until golden, about 10 minutes. Watch them; they burn easily. *Yield: about 40 cheese straws.*

CHEESE ROLL

½ pound Cheddar cheese
2 hard-cooked eggs, chopped
    fine
2 tablespoons minced dill
    pickle
½ cup chopped nuts (pecans
    or walnuts)

½ teaspoon salt
1 teaspoon Worcestershire
    sauce
Few drops Tabasco sauce
    (optional)

Shred or grate the cheese on the coarse side of the grater and mix with the eggs, pickle, nuts, salt, and Worcestershire sauce. Add Tabasco if you wish. Shape into a roll about a foot long. Roll up in plastic wrap or waxed paper and chill. Unwrap, slice into rounds, and serve on round crackers, Melba toast, or pumpernickel rounds. *Serves 8.*

MUSHROOMS FILLED WITH CHEESE

1 pound large mushrooms
5 tablespoons melted butter
3 tablespoons grated Parmesan cheese
½ teaspoon salt
⅛ teaspoon pepper

Remove the stems and wipe the mushrooms. Brush tops with 2 tablespoons of the melted butter. Place mushrooms open side up in a baking dish. Mix the remaining 3 tablespoons butter with the cheese, salt, and pepper, and fill the caps with this mixture. Broil for 8 to 10 minutes, until cheese has melted and the mushrooms are sizzling. Serve on toast if you wish. *Serves 4.*

CHEESE-AND-WINE TOAST

6 slices bread
1 cup white wine
2 eggs, beaten
¾ cup grated Parmesan cheese
3 tablespoons butter

Preheat oven to 350°. Trim the crusts off the bread and cut the slices in half. Dip them one at a time into the wine. Beat the eggs and mix in the cheese. Dip the wine-soaked slices in the mixture, coating them well. Arrange on a well buttered baking sheet and dot with the butter. Bake for 15 minutes, until the bread is browned. Turn the slices and bake five minutes more. Serve hot. *Serves 6.*

STUFFED EGGS

8 eggs, hard-boiled, cooled, and shelled
¼ cup mayonnaise
¼ teaspoon salt
⅛ teaspoon pepper

2 tablespoons grated Parmesan, Parmesan and Romano, or Cheddar cheese
3 slices crisp bacon or 3 teaspoons bacon-flavored bits

Cut each hard-boiled egg in half lengthwise and put the yolks in a bowl. Add mayonnaise, salt, and pepper and mash with a fork. Add the cheese and blend well. Refill the egg whites and sprinkle with the crumbled bacon or bacon-flavored bits. *Serves 4 to 6.*

GERMAN CHEESE BLEND

1 (3 oz.) package cream cheese
½ cup small-curd cottage cheese or pot cheese
2 tablespoons minced onion
½ teaspoon caraway seeds

2 teaspoons capers
1 teaspoon prepared mustard
Pinch salt
1 teaspoon paprika
Cream or white wine (optional)

Mash the cream cheese and cottage or pot cheese together. Stir in the onion, caraway, and capers. Season with mustard, salt, and paprika and blend together thoroughly. If too stiff to handle easily, add a tablespoon of cream or wine. Pack into a mold and refrigerate several hours or overnight. *Serves 4.*

HOT CREAM-CHEESE CHUTNEY

1 (8 oz.) package cream cheese
1 teaspoon grated onion
1 tablespoon lemon juice

2 eggs, slightly beaten
⅓ cup chutney, chopped
Toast rounds

Preheat oven to 450°. Smooth the cheese with the onion and lemon juice, and blend in the slightly beaten eggs. Stir in half the chutney. Put on toast and top with the remaining chutney. Place in oven until hot, about 5 minutes. *Serves 8.*

CAMEMBERT-CHUTNEY SPREAD

4 to 5 ounces Camembert cheese
¼ cup heavy cream

1 teaspoon curry powder
¼ cup chopped chutney

Soften the Camembert to room temperature. Mix the cheese with the cream until smooth. Add curry powder and chutney. *Yield: about 1 cup.*

CREAM CHEESE AND CHUTNEY SPREAD

Proceed as for *Camembert-Chutney Spread* substituting 4 ounces softened cream cheese for the Camembert. *Yield: about 1 cup.*

ROQUEFORT TOAST

2 ounces Roquefort cheese
2 tablespoons tomato paste
Worcestershire sauce

2 slices crisp bacon
4 slices bread

Have the cheese at room temperature. Mash it with a fork. Blend in the tomato paste and Worcestershire sauce to taste. Make squares of toast, 4 to a slice of bread. Spread them with the cheese mixture and heat in the oven for 5 minutes. Sprinkle with the crumbled crisp bacon. *Yield: 16 squares.*

CHEESE DIP

½ cup half-and-half
½ pound Cheddar, grated
1 tablespoon prepared mustard

½ teaspoon salt
1 tablespoon Worcestershire sauce

Have the cheese at room temperature. Put the ingredients in a blender, pouring the half-and-half in first. Buzz at low speed until smooth. *Yield: about 2½ cups.*

CHEESE BALLS

½ pound Camembert or
    Brie cheese
1 cup dry white wine

½ pound butter, softened
1 cup ground blanched
    almonds

Remove the rind from the cheese. Marinate the trimmed cheese in the wine for several hours, turning it twice. Drain. Force the cheese through a food mill, or mash it smooth. Beat in the butter. Chill 3 hours. Form teaspoons of the mixture into balls. Chill the balls, then roll them in the ground almonds. *Yield: about 50.*

CHEESEBURGER CANAPÉS

1 pound lean ground beef
1 cup grated sharp cheese
1 teaspoon salt
¼ teaspoon pepper
1 tablespoon Worcestershire
    sauce

2 tablespoons catchup
½ cup slivered almonds or
    chopped walnuts
Small round buns or tooth-
    picks

Combine all the ingredients except the buns and blend thoroughly with a fork or your fingers. Form loosely into 12 to 16 small patties. Broil them for 2 minutes, turn, and broil 1 minute more. Serve on miniature buns or with toothpicks. These are good with horseradish sauce. *Serves 6 to 8.*

CREAM CHEESE AND CHIPPED BEEF LOG

1 (8 oz.) package cream
   cheese, softened
1 tablespoon horseradish
2 to 3 teaspoons prepared
   mustard

2 (2½ oz.) jars chipped beef
2 tablespoons butter

Mix the softened cheese with horseradish and mustard and chill it. Chop the chipped beef and sauté it in the butter until crisp. Dry on paper toweling. Form the chilled cheese mixture into a log and roll it in the dried beef. Chill again. *Serves 6 to 8.*

soups

Soup's on!—made tasty and succulent with cheese.

CHEESE SOUP

¼ cup minced onions
½ cup grated carrots
¼ cup chopped celery
¼ cup butter
2 tablespoons flour
3 cups chicken broth

½ teaspoon salt
¼ teaspoon pepper
1 cup dry sherry
2 cups (½ lb.) grated
   Cheddar cheese

Sauté the onions, carrots, and celery in butter for 10 minutes, stirring frequently. Blend in the flour; gradually add the broth, stirring steadily. Add the salt and pepper. Simmer for 10 minutes. Stir in the sherry and the cheese, and heat until melted. *Serves 4 to 6.*

CHEDDAR-CHEESE SOUP I

½ cup minced onion
½ cup minced celery
½ cup minced carrots
¼ cup butter
¼ cup flour
4 cups chicken broth
3 cups milk

½ teaspoon salt
¼ teaspoon pepper
1 cup grated Cheddar or process American cheese
Minced parsley (garnish)

Sauté the onion, celery, and carrots in 3 tablespoons of the butter until softened. Add the flour and cook 1 minute. Pour in the broth and milk. When hot and smooth, stir in the salt, pepper, and cheese. Bring to a boil, add the remaining butter, sprinkle with parsley, and serve at once. *Serves 8 to 10.*

CHEDDAR-CHEESE SOUP II

Substitute 2 cups of water and 2 (10½ oz.) cans consommé for the chicken broth in *Cheddar-Cheese Soup I.* Serves 8.

NORWEGIAN CHEESE SOUP

2 cups chopped celery
½ cup chopped green pepper
2 (10¾ oz.) cans cream of mushroom soup
3 cups milk
1 can tomato purée

½ teaspoon pepper
2 cups shredded Cheddar cheese
½ cup sherry
2 tablespoons minced parsley

Cook the celery and pepper in water to cover until tender. Drain and purée in blender. Put the mushroom soup and milk in the top of a double boiler and stir and cook a few minutes. Stir in the puréed vegetables. Add the tomato purée, pepper, and cheese. Cook until smooth. Just before serving, add the sherry and parsley. *Serves 10.*

FRENCH ONION SOUP

4 large onions, sliced
2 tablespoons butter
6 cups beef broth or bouillon
1 teaspoon Worcestershire sauce or ¼ teaspoon Tabasco sauce

6 toasted slices of French bread
Grated Parmesan cheese

In a soup kettle, sauté the onion rings in the butter until they are light brown. Add the broth and the Worcestershire sauce or Tabasco. Cover and simmer until the onions are tender, about 15 minutes. Adjust seasoning. Toast the French bread slices in the oven. When you are ready to serve the soup, divide it into 6 earthenware bowls or other ovenproof dishes. Place a piece of toast on each. Sprinkle with cheese and put under broiler to melt. Or you may pass the toast and cheese separately. *Serves 6.*

ITALIAN MINESTRONE

1 cup white beans or kidney
    beans
2 quarts water
¼ pound salt pork
2 tablespoons olive oil
1 onion, sliced
½ cup diced celery
2 carrots, diced
1 zucchini, diced
1 potato, diced
1 large tomato, peeled and
    diced

2 tablespoons chopped pars-
    ley
1 clove garlic, crushed
2 teaspoons salt
½ teaspoon pepper
½ small head cabbage,
    shredded
1 cup thin macaroni or ver-
    micelli
1 cup grated Parmesan
    cheese

Soak the beans in water to cover overnight, or at least for several hours. Drain them and then simmer for 1 hour in 2 quarts of water with the rind of the pork. Mince the pork and put it in a separate kettle with the oil. Add the onion and cook until softened. Add the celery, carrots, zucchini, potato, tomato, parsley, garlic, salt, and pepper. Add the pork and vegetables to the beans and water, and simmer for 1½ hours. For the last 20 minutes, add the cabbage and the macaroni or vermicelli, broken into small pieces. Just before serving stir in ½ cup of the cheese. The soup should be very thick. Pass more cheese at the table. *Serves 8.*

BOULA

3 pounds fresh peas or 3
    packages frozen peas
1 teaspoon salt
3 (10½ oz.) cans green
    turtle soup
¼ teaspoon pepper

Pinch of mace
Sherry
½ cup heavy cream, whipped
¼ cup grated Parmesan
    cheese

Cook the peas until quite tender in a small amount of water with the salt. If using frozen peas, cook them longer than usual; they should be quite soft. Purée the peas in a blender or press through a sieve. Heat the soup with the purée of peas but do not let it boil. Add the pepper and mace and a little sherry to taste. Be careful not to overpower the turtle flavor with sherry. Pour into individual casseroles or a large one, top with dollops of whipped cream, and sprinkle with the cheese. Place under the broiler for about 3 minutes, until the cream and cheese are slightly browned. Serve at once. *Serves 8.*

main dishes

Money-saving *main dishes* result from the generous use of cheese.

FILLETS OF SOLE AU GRATIN

1 cup dry white wine
2 tablespoons butter
2 tablespoons grated onion
½ cup chopped mushrooms
2 teaspoons chopped parsley
3 tablespoons heavy cream

1 tablespoon salt
½ teaspoon pepper
2 pounds fillets of sole
3 tablespoons grated Parmesan cheese

Preheat oven to 350°. Combine the wine, butter, onion, mushrooms, and parsley in a saucepan. Simmer 10 minutes. Mix in the cream. Sprinkle the salt and pepper on the fillets. Arrange them in a large buttered baking dish in a single layer. Pour the sauce over them and top with the cheese. Bake for 25 minutes. *Serves 4 to 6.*

SEA FOOD, MUSHROOM, AND NOODLE CASSEROLE

1 pound cooked, shelled
   shrimps
1 cup cooked lobster or crab
   meat
2 cups cooked noodles
1 clove garlic, crushed
½ pound mushrooms, sliced

6 tablespoons butter
3 tablespoons flour
1½ cups milk
1 cup grated Cheddar cheese
1 teaspoon salt
1 teaspoon pepper
2 teaspoons lemon juice

Cook the noodles according to package directions, and drain. Sauté the garlic and mushrooms in 3 tablespoons of the butter for 2 to 3 minutes. Add the shrimps and the lobster or crab. In another pan, melt the remaining butter, stir in the flour, and add the milk gradually while stirring. When this sauce is smooth and thickened, add ¾ cup of the cheese and stir until melted. Add the salt, pepper, and lemon juice. Pour over the sea food and mix lightly. Put the noodles in a 1½-quart casserole, and pour the sauce and fish over them. Top with remaining cheese and broil until the cheese is bubbling. If you have done this much ahead of time and the casserole is cold when you put it in the oven, heat it at 350° for 15 minutes and then broil. *Serves 6.*

SWISS CHICKEN BREASTS IN FOIL

3 double or 6 single chicken
   breasts
½ cup butter
1 teaspoon salt
¼ teaspoon pepper

¼ cup minced parsley
2 tablespoons minced scallions or 1 tablespoon
   minced chives
6 slices Swiss cheese

Preheat oven to 400°. Cut the breasts in half if you have double ones, rub them with butter and dust with salt and pepper. Place each half chicken breast on a piece of foil about 10 inches square. Sprinkle with parsley and scallions or chives, and top with the cheese. Fold the foil loosely over each breast; be sure the ends and edges are sealed. Bake for 45 minutes. *Serves 6.*

CHICKEN OR TURKEY TETRAZZINI

4 cups cooked turkey or chicken, diced
1 pound spaghetti
2 cups water
2 cups chicken broth or 2 chicken-bouillon cubes dissolved in 2 cups of water

1½ pounds mushrooms, sliced
6 tablespoons butter
1 clove garlic, crushed
4 tablespoons flour
½ cup heavy cream
½ cup grated Parmesan cheese

Cook the spaghetti in half water and half chicken broth until barely tender. Drain and reserve the broth. Brown the mushrooms and garlic in 4 tablespoons of the butter. Remove them and set aside. Add 2 tablespoons butter and blend in the flour; add 3 cups of the broth the spaghetti was cooked in and the cream. Cook and stir until smooth and thickened. Put a layer of ⅓ of the spaghetti in the bottom of a large casserole, cover with ⅓ of the turkey or chicken and a layer of mushrooms, and add ⅓ of the cream sauce. Sprinkle with Parmesan cheese. Repeat twice more, ending with cream sauce on top. Sprinkle with the remaining Parmesan cheese. Bake at 450° until bubbling and browned on top. *Serves 8.*

If you have a huge casserole, double the recipe for 14 to 16 people; if not, make two.

TURKEY OR CHICKEN DIVAN

Slices of cooked turkey or chicken breast
2 pounds asparagus or 1 bunch broccoli
¼ cup butter
¼ cup flour
2 cups milk or half-and-half
1 teaspoon salt
¼ teaspoon white pepper
1 cup grated Parmesan cheese

Cook the asparagus or broccoli in salted water until tender. Place in a very shallow ovenproof dish or platter. Cover completely with sliced turkey or chicken. To make the cream sauce, melt the butter over low heat. Blend in the flour; do not let it brown. Add the milk or half-and-half gradually while stirring. Add the salt and pepper and cook until smooth and thickened. Add ½ cup of the cheese, stir until the cheese melts, and then pour the sauce over the chicken or turkey. Sprinkle remaining cheese on top and slide the dish under the broiler. When the sauce bubbles and is lightly browned, serve at once. *Serves 6.*

If you are serving 12, it is easier to make two casseroles for 6 each.

LONDON BROIL WITH BLUE CHEESE

⅓ cup white wine vinegar
⅓ cup water
2 tablespoons soy sauce
1 onion, sliced
1 clove garlic, mashed
½ teaspoon salt
¼ teaspoon pepper
2 flank or chuck steaks (about 2½ lbs.)
¼ cup crumbled blue cheese

To make the marinade, combine the vinegar, water, soy sauce, onion, garlic, salt, and pepper. Score steaks lightly on both sides and marinate them several hours or overnight, turning occasionally. Place steaks under the broiler or broil them over coals for about 5 minutes. Turn and sprinkle the uncooked side with blue cheese. Broil this second side 5 minutes. Place on a platter, and slice into thin diagonal slices across the grain. *Serves 4.*

ROQUEFORT HAMBURGER STEAK

2½ to 3 pounds ground beef ⅓ pound Roquefort cheese
½ teaspoon salt 2 tablespoons cream
½ teaspoon pepper

Mix the beef, salt, and pepper, and form into 6 patties about 1 inch thick. Smooth the Roquefort with the cream and place some in the center of each patty. Seal the edges with a little water. Broil on each side to desired degree of doneness. *Serves 6.*

HAMBURGER STEAK WITH CHEDDAR CHEESE

2½ to 3 pounds ground beef 2 tablespoons butter
1 teaspoon salt 6 slices Cheddar cheese
¼ teaspoon pepper

Mix the beef, salt, and pepper and form into six loose patties about 1 inch thick. Do not squash the patties down. Sauté in hot butter for 1 minute on one side, turn, and sauté 2 minutes more. Place a slice of Cheddar on each and broil until the cheese melts. *Serves 6.*

TOMATO CHEESEBURGERS

Put a slice of tomato under the cheese used in *Hamburger Steak with Cheddar Cheese.*

VEAL PARMIGIANA

8 veal scallops (thin cutlets, about 3 pounds altogether)
1 cup toasted bread crumbs
1 cup grated Parmesan cheese
1 teaspoon salt
¼ teaspoon pepper
Flour
2 eggs, beaten
3 tablespoons olive oil
Thin slices Mozzarella cheese, about 1 pound

Have the veal scallops pounded flat, or pound them yourself. Place each one between 2 pieces of waxed paper and use a rolling pin or the bottom of a heavy water glass or bottle. Mix the crumbs, Parmesan cheese, ½ teaspoon of the salt, and pepper. Add the remaining salt to the flour and roll the pieces of veal in it. Then turn them in the eggs, and lastly in the crumb mixture. Sauté the veal in oil for a few minutes on each side. Place them in a flat pan, top with the Mozzarella, and bake at 350° for about 15 minutes, or until the cheese is melted. Brown for a minute under the broiler. *Serves 8.*

CHEESE SOUFFLÉ

4 tablespoons butter
4 tablespoons flour
1 teaspoon salt
Pinch cayenne pepper
1½ cups milk
½ pound sharp Cheddar cheese, shredded
6 eggs, separated

Blend the butter, salt, and cayenne, and stir in the milk. When smooth add the cheese and cook and stir until melted. Cool slightly while beating the egg yolks. Stir in the beaten egg yolks. Whip the egg whites until stiff and fold in. Bake in an ungreased 2-quart casserole, filling it ½ to ⅔ full. Bake at 300° for 1¼ hours. Serve immediately. *Serves 4 to 6.*

CHEESE SOUFFLÉ WITH BACON

¼ cup butter
3 tablespoons flour
1½ cups evaporated milk
6 ounces Cheddar cheese,
    cut into small pieces

4 eggs
¼ teaspoon salt
5 slices crisp bacon

Preheat oven to 350°. Melt the butter and blend in the flour. Add the milk slowly while stirring. Stir in the cheese and keep stirring until the sauce is smooth. Beat the egg yolks slightly. Add some hot cheese sauce to them; then return the yolks to the cheese mixture carefully, stirring constantly. Cook slowly for 1 to 2 minutes until thickened. Remove from heat. Beat the egg whites with salt until stiff. Crumble the bacon and fold it into the whites. Then fold the whites into the cheese mixture and pour into a greased 1½-quart soufflé dish. Bake about 40 minutes. The soufflé should be puffed up and golden on top but quite soft in the center. Serve at once. *Serves 4.*

RICE-AND-CHEESE CASSEROLE

1½ cups rice
3 cups water
1 teaspoon salt
¼ cup butter
⅓ pound mild Cheddar
    cheese, shredded

Milk
Buttered bread or cracker
    crumbs

Put the rice, water, salt, and 1 tablespoon of the butter in a heavy pot or skillet. Bring to a boil, reduce heat, cover, and cook for 15 minutes. Do not stir. Preheat the oven to 350°. Rake ⅓ of the rice into a buttered casserole, using a fork; a spoon will mash the grains. Add a third of the cheese. Repeat twice. Pour

milk up to half the depth of the rice-cheese mixture.
Top with crumbs and dot with the remaining butter.
Bake until the cheese melts and the crumbs are brown,
about 20 minutes. *Serves 6.*

CHEESE FONDUE CASSEROLE

1 cup milk
1 cup bread crumbs
1 tablespoon butter
¼ pound mild cheese,
    shredded

3 eggs, separated
½ teaspoon salt

Preheat oven to 350°. Mix the milk, bread crumbs,
butter, and cheese in a saucepan and cook and stir until
the cheese melts and the mixture is smooth. Remove
from heat. Beat the egg yolks until thick and add them
to the cheese mixture. Add the salt to the whites and
beat until stiff. Fold them into the cheese mixture and
spoon into a buttered 1-quart baking dish. Bake for 20
to 25 minutes. *Serves 6.*

BAKED CHEESE CASSEROLE

8 slices bread (no crusts)
Soft butter
2 cups shredded Cheddar
    cheese
6 eggs, beaten

3 cups milk
1 teaspoon salt
¼ teaspoon pepper
2 teaspoons prepared mus-
    tard

Preheat oven to 350°. Spread the bread lightly with
the butter. Cut it into 4 squares per slice. Put half the
bread in the bottom of a greased baking dish or casserole (about 2-quart size). Put half the cheese on the
bread. Add the remaining bread and cheese. Mix the

beaten eggs, milk, salt, pepper, and mustard. Pour over the bread and cheese. Bake for about an hour, until set and browned on top. *Serves 6.*

CHEESE-AND-WINE BREAD CASSEROLE

6 slices stale white bread
¼ cup soft butter
3 eggs
½ cup chicken broth
1 cup dry white wine
½ teaspoon salt

¼ teaspoon pepper
2 teaspoons Worcestershire sauce
2 cups grated Swiss-type cheese

Preheat oven to 350°. Butter the bread and cut it into strips. Line a baking dish with the bread, butter side down. Beat the eggs. Add the broth, wine, salt, pepper, and Worcestershire sauce. Beat again thoroughly and beat in the cheese gradually. Pour into the casserole. Bake for about 25 minutes. *Serves 6.*

CHEESE BROCHETTES

6 slices bread (crusts off)
1 cup milk
3 eggs, beaten

20 pieces Mozzarella cheese, cut ¼″ thick
3 tablespoons melted butter

Cut the bread in quarters and pour the milk over it. Let stand a few minutes, then drain. Dip the bread in the beaten eggs. Thread on brochettes, alternating with the pieces of cheese. Put the brochettes into an open pan, pour the butter over them, and bake at 400° for about 15 minutes, or until browned. *Serves 6.*

FRIED CHEESE CAKES

1 pound small-curd cottage
    cheese
2 eggs, beaten
½ teaspoon salt
¼ teaspoon white pepper

1 tablespoon flour
Butter
Powdered sugar (optional)
Sour cream (optional)

Mix the cheese with the beaten eggs. Season with salt and pepper and stir in the flour. Form into round cakes about 1 inch thick. Fry on a hot buttered griddle, turning once. They should be golden, not dark brown. Sprinkle with a little powdered sugar and serve with sour cream, if you wish. *Serves 4.*

CHEESE DUMPLINGS

½ pound ricotta or small-
    curd cottage cheese
2 tablespoons butter
1 egg, slightly beaten
½ teaspoon salt

¼ teaspoon pepper
Flour
1 quart chicken or beef broth
Grated Parmesan cheese
Melted butter

Mix the ricotta or cottage cheese with the softened butter, the slightly beaten egg, and the salt and pepper. Form into small balls and dust with flour. Drop a few at a time into the boiling broth. When they come to the surface, they are done. Serve with grated cheese and melted butter. *Serves 6.*

CHEESE-AND-TOMATO PIE

4 cups croutons
3 large tomatoes
1 pound Swiss cheese,
    shredded

3 eggs
2 cups milk
1 teaspoon salt
½ teaspoon pepper

Put the croutons in the bottom of a 9-inch pie plate or casserole. Peel and slice the tomatoes thin and place the slices over the croutons. Cover with the cheese. Set aside. Beat the eggs with the milk, salt, and pepper. About 45 minutes before serving, pour the egg mixture over all and bake at 350° until browned on top and puffy. *Serves 6.*

QUICHE LORRAINE

9-inch Unbaked Pie Shell
2 tablespoons soft butter
12 slices bacon
⅓ cup shredded Swiss
    cheese

4 eggs
2 cups cream
Pinch salt

Preheat oven to 425°. Spread the pie crust with the butter. Fry the bacon until crisp; drain and crumble it. Sprinkle the cheese and bacon on the crust. Beat the eggs with the cream and salt, using a rotary beater. Pour over the cheese-bacon mixture. Bake at 425° to 450° for 15 minutes, then reduce to 350° and bake until set, about half an hour more. *Serves 6.*

PIZZA

2 frozen pizza-pie crusts or
    2 **9-inch Baked Pie
    Shells**
¾ cup canned tomatoes
1 to 2 cloves garlic, crushed
¼ teaspoon oregano

1 small can anchovies, cut up
½ cup ham or salami,
    chopped
½ pound Mozzarella cheese,
    sliced thin

Heat the frozen pizzas according to directions and put them into pie pans. If you use *Baked Shells,* leave them in the pans. Mix the tomatoes, garlic, and oregano, and spread over the crust. Dot with pieces of anchovy and ham or salami. Cover with slices of cheese. Just before serving, heat under the broiler until the cheese bubbles. *Serves 6 to 8.*

OLIVE OR MUSHROOM PIZZA

1 package hot-roll mix
Flour
1 tablespoon salad or olive oil
1 (8 oz.) can tomato sauce
½ teaspoon oregano
1 cup pitted black olives, chopped, or 1 cup sliced mushrooms

4 ounces thinly sliced ham or prosciutto, cut into 1-inch squares; or salami strips or anchovy strips
1½ cups grated sharp Cheddar cheese or thin slices Mozzarella cheese (about ½ pound)

Prepare hot-roll mix as directed on the package. Cover and let rise in a warm place until doubled in bulk. Turn dough out onto a floured board and roll into a rectangle as thin as you possibly can. Place dough on a greased baking pan which has a 1-inch rim and pull the edges up. If you have a large pizza pan, roll the dough into a circle and fit as directed. Brush dough with oil and spread tomato sauce evenly over the surface. Sprinkle with oregano, olives or mushrooms, and the ham or salami or anchovy strips. Sprinkle Cheddar cheese over all or cover with Mozzarella cheese. Bake at 400° about 20 minutes. Cut and serve warm. *Serves 6 to 8.*

pasta

Pasta comes in many shapes and sizes, under many names, and every single one of them is economical and delicious. In Italy pasta is the staple of life. The Italians like it cooked "to the teeth" (*al dente,* firm), and dressed to the teeth with cheese.

SPAGHETTINI AND MEAT BALLS

2 medium onions, chopped
4 tablespoons olive oil
2 pounds lean ground beef
3 eggs, slightly beaten
1 cup bread crumbs
2 tablespoons chopped
    parsley

1 cup grated Parmesan
    cheese (or Parmesan
    and Romano)
2 teaspoons salt
1 teaspoon pepper
2 cups tomato sauce
1 pound spaghettini

Sauté the onions in 1 tablespoon of the oil until soft but not brown. Put the meat in a bowl with 1 more tablespoon oil, the slightly beaten eggs, the bread crumbs, parsley, and ½ cup of the cheese. Mix and stir in the onions, salt, and pepper. Blend thoroughly and form into balls. Sauté in remaining oil, browning on all sides. Add the tomato sauce and simmer covered for 20 minutes. Cook the spaghettini *al dente,* and drain. Serve on a hot platter topped with meat balls and sauce. Pass remaining cheese. *Serves 6.*

SPAGHETTI WITH KIDNEYS

1 clove garlic, crushed
¼ pound butter
2 pounds veal or lamb kidneys, cleaned, cored, and sliced very thin
2 tablespoons flour
½ teaspoon black pepper
1½ teaspoons salt

6 anchovy fillets, drained and minced
Juice of ½ lemon
½ teaspoon oregano
1 tablespoon chopped parsley
1 pound spaghetti
½ cup grated cheese

Sauté the garlic in the butter. Dust kidneys lightly with the flour, salt, and pepper, and sauté for 1 minute on each side. Stir in the anchovies; add the lemon juice, oregano, and parsley; blend. Simmer for 5 minutes, breaking up the anchovies. Cook the spaghetti *al dente*; drain. Place it in a large hot bowl, top with cheese, toss, and pour kidney sauce over it. Toss again. *Serves 6.*

SPAGHETTI CHEESE PIE

¾ pound spaghetti or spaghettini
6 slices bacon
1 onion, chopped
¾ pound Cheddar cheese, grated or shredded

3 eggs
1 cup milk
1 teaspoon salt
¼ teaspoon pepper
1 teaspoon Worcestershire sauce

Cook the spaghetti *al dente*. Meanwhile, sauté the bacon. Remove the bacon and pour off some of the grease, leaving about 2 tablespoons. Add the onion and cook 1 to 2 minutes. Cut the bacon into pieces and add. Mix 2 cups of the cheese into the drained hot spaghetti. Then combine the bacon mixture with the spaghetti and put into a greased 1-quart casserole. Beat the eggs, milk, salt, pepper, and Worcestershire sauce together and stir in the remaining cheese. Pour this sauce over the spaghetti and bake uncovered at 325° for half an hour. *Serves 4 to 6.*

SPAGHETTINI WITH BABY SQUID

12 baby squid
3 tablespoons olive oil
1 clove garlic, minced
4 cups (2 lb. can) Italian plum tomatoes
2 tablespoons minced parsley
1 pound spaghettini

Clean the squid, removing the bones, which lift out like pieces of plastic. Split, wash away the gelatinous matter, and rinse. Cut into pieces straight across. Heat the oil and sauté the squid and garlic in it until the squid pieces curl. Add the tomatoes and parsley, stir, and simmer, uncovered, for 15 minutes, until the sauce thickens and the pieces of squid become fork-tender. Cook the spaghettini *al dente*; drain well. Serve in hot soup bowls with squid sauce spooned over. *Serves 6.*

LINGUINE WITH RED CLAM SAUCE

3 small onions, chopped
1 garlic clove, minced
3 tablespoons olive oil
1 (2 lb.) can Italian plum tomatoes
1 teaspoon salt
¼ teaspoon black pepper
1 teaspoon oregano
4 anchovies, chopped
1 (10½ oz.) can minced clams
1 pound linguine
½ pound Parmesan cheese, grated

Sauté the onions and garlic in the oil until onions are soft. Add the tomatoes, and simmer for 10 minutes. Add the salt, pepper, oregano, and anchovies; cover and simmer for 10 minutes more. Add the clams with their juice; stir well, and simmer, uncovered, until the sauce thickens. Cook the linguine *al dente,* drain, and place in a warm bowl. Toss in half the cheese. Pour in half the sauce; toss well, but gently. Serve in hot soup bowls with the rest of the sauce and cheese spooned over. *Serves 4 to 6.*

LINGUINE WITH WHITE CLAM SAUCE

1 clove garlic, crushed
⅓ cup olive oil
½ cup clam juice
¼ teaspoon salt
¼ teaspoon black pepper
⅓ teaspoon dried oregano

1 can (7½ oz.) minced clams
2 tablespoons chopped Italian parsley
1 pound linguine
½ cup grated Parmesan cheese

Sauté the garlic in the oil for 2 minutes. Add the clam juice, salt, pepper, and oregano; simmer for 5 minutes. Add the clams with the liquid in the can, stir in well, and cook, uncovered, so that the sauce will reduce, about 8 minutes. Stir in the parsley and mix well. Cook the linguine *al dente,* drain, and toss well with half of the clam sauce. Serve the remainder spooned over, and top with cheese. *Serves 4 to 6.*

LINGUINE AND CHOPPED BEEF

2½ pounds lean ground beef
½ pound ripe Gorgonzola cheese

1 teaspoon salt
5 tablespoons butter
1 pound linguine

Make 7 meat patties 2 inches thick. In the center of each bury a 1-inch cube of Gorgonzola cheese. Pinch the edges of beef together. Sprinkle with salt. Sauté the patties in 2 tablespoons of the butter, turning until they are brown outside but still pink inside and the cheese is melted. This takes about 10 minutes. Remove 6 of the patties to a warm plate. Crumble the other patty in the pan, stirring the meat well into the browned butter in the pan, and adding remaining butter. Cook the linguine in rapidly boiling salted water until *al dente,* drain, and toss with the crumbled meat mixture. Add the beef-cheese patties. *Serves 6.*

LINGUINE FINE WITH TOMATO AND SHRIMP

3 white onions, chopped
1 clove garlic, crushed
3 tablespoons olive oil
8 large ripe tomatoes or 1 (2 lb.) can Italian tomatoes
2 teaspoons salt
1 teaspoon sugar
1 cup dry white wine
1 pound raw shrimps, shelled
2 tablespoons chopped parsley
1 pound linguine fine

Cook the onions and garlic in the oil until soft. Peel the tomatoes, cut them into pieces, or use canned tomatoes, and add them to the onions with the salt and sugar. Simmer for 20 minutes. In another pan bring the wine to a boil; drop in the shrimps and simmer for 3 minutes. If the shrimps are large, cut them in half lengthwise. Add wine and shrimps to the tomato sauce. Stir in the parsley and cook for 5 minutes. Cook the linguine *al dente,* drain, and place in a warm bowl. Pour half of the sauce over and toss. Top with remaining sauce and some shrimps. *Serves 6.*

FETTUCCINE ALFREDO

1 pound fettuccine
¼ pound butter, cut up
¾ cup grated Parmesan
    cheese

¼ cup heavy cream, warmed

Cook the fettuccine *al dente*. Drain and put on a hot serving dish or platter, or in a chafing dish. Add the butter and cheese and toss. Add cream and toss thoroughly. *Serves 4 to 6.*

FETTUCCINE WITH FISH

2 tablespoons butter
2 tablespoons olive oil
3 small onions, chopped
1 clove garlic, minced
1 small green pepper,
    chopped
1 (2 oz.) can anchovies,
    chopped

½ teaspoon black pepper
1 cup tomato sauce
1 cup dry white wine
½ teaspoon tarragon
1 pound medium cod or had-
    dock fillets, cut into
    bite-size pieces
1 pound fettuccine

Heat the butter and oil in a heavy cooking pot. Add the onions, garlic, green pepper, anchovies with their oil, and black pepper. Sauté until the vegetables are soft. Stir in the tomato sauce; then add the tarragon and the pieces of fish. Simmer, uncovered, until the fish is tender but not falling apart, about 10 minutes. Cook the fettuccine *al dente,* drain, and toss gently with half of the fish sauce, using forks. Serve in a hot bowl. Top with the remaining sauce. *Serves 4 to 6.*

ELBOW MACARONI AND CHEESE CASSEROLE

½ pound elbow macaroni	3 eggs
¼ pound Cheddar cheese, shredded	1 cup milk
½ pound bacon	1 teaspoon salt

Preheat oven to 350°. Cook the macaroni *al dente*. Drain and fold in half the cheese. Meanwhile, cut the bacon in ¼-inch pieces and fry until crisp. Beat the eggs, milk, and salt together. Add half the remaining cheese. Pile the macaroni-cheese mixture into a greased shallow casserole. Pour the egg mixture over it and top with the remaining cheese and bacon. Bake until hot and the cheese is melted, about 20 minutes. *Serves 4.*

MUSHROOM-AND-NOODLE CASSEROLE

1 pound small mushrooms	1½ cups heavy cream
½ cup butter	3 tablespoons flour
¼ cup minced onion	¾ pound medium noodles
1 teaspoon salt	¼ cup grated Parmesan cheese
¼ teaspoon pepper	
½ cup dry white wine	

Preheat oven to 400°. If the mushrooms are small, leave them whole; otherwise cut them in half. Melt 2 tablespoons of the butter and sauté the onions until transparent but not brown, add the mushrooms and cook 3 to 4 minutes. Add the salt, pepper, and wine and simmer covered for 5 minutes. Add the cream. Blend 3 more tablespoons of the butter with the flour and blend into the sauce. Cook the noodles according to package directions. Drain and toss in the remaining butter. Put into a casserole. Pour the sauce over it. Stir gently, sprinkle with the cheese, and bake about 20 minutes. *Serves 4 to 6.*

NOODLES WITH COTTAGE CHEESE

1 pound medium noodles
1 pound large-curd cottage
  cheese
1 pint sour cream

½ cup grated Parmesan
  cheese
2 tablespoons butter

Cook the noodles in salted water according to package directions. Drain thoroughly. Put a layer in the bottom of a baking dish, cover with a layer of cottage cheese, and then with a layer of sour cream and a sprinkling of Parmesan cheese. Repeat until the dish is full, making at least 3 layers of noodles. End with a layer of the Parmesan cheese on top and dot with butter. Bake at 350° for 20 minutes. *Serves 6.*

eggs

Eggs get along cordially with cheese.

CHEESE OMELET

6 eggs
2 tablespoons water or cream
¼ teaspoon salt
⅛ teaspoon pepper
⅛ teaspoon fines herbes
  (optional)

2 to 3 tablespoons butter
2 ounces Cheddar cheese,
  shredded
1 tablespoon grated Parmesan cheese

Beat the eggs slightly with a fork and add the water or cream; water makes a tenderer omelet. Season with salt and pepper, and the fines herbes if you wish. You may wait to salt and pepper the eggs until just before they're finished. There is a theory that salt toughens eggs. Put about 2 tablespoons of butter into a hot 10-inch omelet pan and let it sizzle but not brown. Swish the butter onto the sides of the pan. Pour in the eggs, lower the heat, shake the pan with one hand and stir with a fork in the other; let some of the egg run under the edges. When the eggs begin to set, stop stirring for a minute, until the bottom is firm but not brown and the top is still creamy. Put the Cheddar cheese in the center. Quickly loosen the omelet around the edges, tip the pan, and then fold the omelet over in half with a spatula or pancake turner. Slide it onto a warm plate, folding once more as you slip the omelet onto the plate. Rub the top with a piece of butter for a moment if you wish, and sprinkle the Parmesan cheese on top. *Serves 2 or 3.*

TOMATO-CHEESE OMELET

3 eggs
½ teaspoon salt
Pinch of pepper
½ teaspoon fines herbes
2 tablespoons grated Parmesan, or ¼ cup finely diced Swiss or Cheddar cheese

½ cup chopped, peeled, and seeded tomatoes
2 tablespoons milk or water (optional)
2 tablespoons butter

Beat the eggs with the salt and pepper using a fork; (no machinery), add the fines herbes and cheese. You may also add 2 tablespoons of milk or water if you wish. Melt the butter in an omelet pan until it foams;

then pour the tomatoes into the foaming butter and add the egg mixture. Stir as for scrambled eggs until almost set but still soft. Stop stirring, shake the pan with your left hand, and with a fork or spatula raise the eggs from the edges to let any loose trickles run under. Shut off heat and let stand about ½ minute. Fold the omelet over with a spatula, then tilt the pan over a warm plate and turn it out, making another fold. *Serves 1.*

SCRAMBLED EGGS WITH PARMESAN CHEESE

8 eggs
½ teaspoon salt
2 tablespoons warm water
    (optional)

½ cup grated Parmesan
    cheese
2 tablespoons butter

Beat the eggs and salt, and water if you wish, with a fork. Add the cheese. Heat the butter in a frying pan but do not brown it. Pour in the eggs and reduce the heat. Stir gently with a fork or spoon. When the eggs are still quite soft, turn off the heat and continue to stir until they are the consistency you want. *Serves 4.*

SCRAMBLED EGGS WITH COTTAGE CHEESE

8 eggs
1 teaspoon salt
2 tablespoons milk
⅛ teaspoon pepper

2 tablespoons butter
½ cup creamed cottage
    cheese

Beat together the eggs, salt, milk, and pepper, using a fork. Melt the butter. When it is foaming but not brown, pour in the egg mixture and reduce the heat. Cook slowly, stirring gently. When the mixture begins to set, fold in the cottage cheese and continue cooking until the eggs are firm but soft. *Serves 4.*

SHIRRED EGGS WITH CHEESE

2 eggs
1 tablespoon butter
Buttered crumbs (optional)

Pinch salt
Pinch pepper
1 slice Cheddar cheese

Butter a ramekin or small ovenproof baking dish. Sprinkle with a few buttered crumbs if you wish. Break in the eggs and top with salt, pepper, and cheese. Bake at 325° for 10 to 15 minutes until the cheese melts and the whites are set. *Serves 1.*

SHIRRED EGGS GRUYÈRE

Substitute sliced Gruyère cheese for the Cheddar in *Shirred Eggs with Cheese.*

POACHED EGGS WITH CHEESE SAUCE

2 tablespoons butter
¼ cup flour
2 cups milk
½ teaspoon salt
¼ teaspoon pepper
½ cup heavy cream

⅓ cup grated Parmesan
   cheese
2 teaspoons Dijon mustard
8 eggs
Bread crumbs

Melt the butter, stir in the flour, and when blended, stir in the milk slowly. Cook and stir until thickened. Add the salt, pepper, cream, cheese, and mustard. Cook and stir until blended. Meanwhile, poach the eggs. Put a little sauce in each of 8 ramekins or 4 cocottes. Put an egg in each ramekin or 2 eggs each in the larger dishes. Sprinkle very lightly with crumbs and place under the broiler for 1 minute. Serve at once. *Serves 8 as a first course or 4 as a main dish.*

vegetables

Sauced or sprinkled with cheese, vegetables become an important part of the meal.

ASPARAGUS JUDGE TRUAX

3 pounds heavy asparagus	⅓ cup grated Parmesan
6 slices Smithfield or other	cheese
cooked ham	6 eggs
Juice of 1 lemon	½ teaspoon salt
¼ cup melted butter	Freshly ground pepper

Clean the asparagus, scraping the lower third. Cook in salted water, or steam until tender. Arrange the ham slices in the bottom of a flat baking dish. Divide the asparagus into six portions and place one on each slice of ham. Sprinkle with lemon juice and 3 tablespoons of the melted butter. Sprinkle with a little cheese and place under the broiler for a few minutes while you fry the eggs in the remaining butter. Place an egg on each portion of asparagus. Sprinkle with salt and pepper and the remaining cheese. Return to the broiler for 2 minutes, or until the cheese is light brown. *Serves 6.*

STUFFED ARTICHOKES

6 artichokes
1 tablespoon salt
1 tablespoon vinegar
1 cup chopped onions
½ cup butter

⅓ cup bread crumbs
¼ teaspoon pepper
½ cup grated Parmesan
  cheese

Trim the tips of the artichoke leaves with scissors if you wish, cutting off ¼ to ½ inch. This improves their looks, not the taste. Put them into a large kettle with water to cover. Add the salt and vinegar and cook for about half an hour. To test for doneness, pull out a leaf; if it comes out easily, the artichokes are cooked. Drain them upside down. Meanwhile, sauté the onions in ¼ cup butter until clear but not browned. Mix the onions with the bread crumbs, pepper, cheese, and the remaining butter, melted. Spread the artichoke leaves apart. Scrape out the tiny center leaves and the choke. Stuff the artichokes with the onion mixture. Tie the leaves up if necessary; they may stay up if pushed into place. Place the artichokes in a greased baking dish and heat at 350° for 15 to 20 minutes. *Serves 6.*

BRAISED ENDIVE

8 to 16 heads Belgian endive
2 to 3 cups consommé
2 teaspoons flour

¼ cup grated Parmesan
  cheese

If the endive heads are small you will need 2 per person. Wash them and trim away all the brown stems. Be careful not to cut too close or the leaves will fall off. Place the endive in a shallow pan with consommé almost to cover. Simmer until tender, about 20 minutes. Drain and place on a warm dish. Boil the broth rapidly until it is reduced to 1 cup; thicken it with the flour, and pour it over the endive. Sprinkle with cheese. *Serves 8.*

CAULIFLOWER POLONAISE

1 large head or 2 small heads cauliflower	½ cup bread crumbs
	¼ cup butter
Salt	¼ cup grated cheese

Cook the cauliflower in salted water to cover, or steam over boiling water until just tender but not too soft; about half an hour should do it. Drain. Meanwhile, sauté the crumbs in the butter until lightly browned. Sprinkle the crumbs with the cheese and reheat. Put the cauliflower on a warm platter and pour the very hot cheese-crumbs over it. *Serves 6.*

CARROT CASSEROLE

4 cups sliced or diced carrots	1 medium onion, minced
Salt	1 cup diced Cheddar cheese
½ cup water	Crumbs, corn flakes, or
¼ cup butter, melted	potato chips

Preheat oven to 350°. Cook the carrots for 5 to 6 minutes in salted water. Drain them and put them into a casserole. Add the butter, onions, and cheese, and stir. Top with crumbs, corn flakes, or crushed potato chips. Bake for 20 minutes. *Serves 6.*

GREEN BEANS AU GRATIN

2 packages frozen French-cut green beans
2 tablespoons butter
2 tablespoons flour
1 cup cream or sour cream
1½ cups grated Cheddar cheese
Crumbs or cornflakes (optional)
Butter

Preheat oven to 350°. Cook the beans according to package directions but undercook them, since they will be cooked again. Melt the butter, stir in the flour, remove from heat, and add the cream. Combine with the beans and half of the cheese. Pour into a casserole and sprinkle the remaining cheese on top. Add crumbs or cornflakes if you wish and top with a few dots of butter. Bake until heated through, about 25 minutes. *Serves 6.*

SPINACH PIE

Unbaked 9-inch Pie Shell
2 packages frozen chopped spinach
4 eggs
1 (3 oz.) package cream cheese
¼ cup shredded Cheddar cheese
½ teaspoon rosemary
½ clove garlic, crushed
½ teaspoon salt
2 tablespoons grated Parmesan cheese

Preheat oven to 450°. Put the pastry in a pie plate, flute the edges, and bake for 10 minutes. Remove pastry and lower oven heat to 400°. Meanwhile cook spinach according to package directions and drain. Beat the eggs with the cream cheese and Cheddar cheese. Stir into the spinach. Add the rosemary, garlic, and salt. Pour into the pie shell. Top with the Parmesan cheese and bake at 400° for 15 to 20 minutes. *Serves 8.*

BAKED SPINACH AND CHEESE

2 packages frozen chopped
    spinach
2 tablespoons minced onion
2 tablespoons butter

1 cup sour cream
½ cup grated Cheddar
    cheese

Preheat oven to 350°. Cook the spinach, following package directions; but cook it a little less since it will be cooked again. Drain it. Sauté the onion in the butter and combine it with the spinach and sour cream. Pour into a baking dish and top with the cheese. Bake until hot and the cheese melts, about 20 minutes. *Serves 6.*

BROILED ONIONS

2 pounds medium-size onions
¼ cup butter
3 tablespoons flour
1½ cups milk

½ teaspoon salt
¼ teaspoon pepper
1 cup grated or shredded
    Cheddar cheese

Parboil the onions for 2 to 3 minutes in salted water. Drain and place them in a shallow ovenproof dish.

Make the sauce by melting 3 tablespoons of the butter; add the flour and when smooth, stir in the milk gradually over low heat. Season with the salt and pepper, add the cheese, and cook and stir until melted and smooth. Add the remaining butter, pour over the onions, and broil for about 10 minutes until hot and lightly browned on top. *Serves 8.*

BAKED CREAMED ONIONS

2 (1 lb.) cans small onions or 2 pounds small white onions
1 cup half-and-half
⅓ cup dry sherry
½ teaspoon salt
¼ cup butter
⅓ cup grated Cheddar cheese

If using fresh onions, peel and boil them in salted water until tender. Drain the onions and put them into a shallow baking dish. Pour the half-and-half and sherry over them, add salt, and dot with butter. Sprinkle with the cheese and bake at 350° for about 25 minutes. *Serves 6.*

STUFFED POTATOES

8 medium potatoes or 4 very large ones
½ cup hot half-and-half
1 tablespoon butter
¼ cup grated Parmesan or crumbled Roquefort cheese
1½ teaspoons salt
¼ teaspoon pepper

Preheat oven to 400°. Scrub the potatoes. Bake them for about 45 minutes. The potatoes should be soft. You may prick the skins with a fork to let the steam out. Roll them back and forth on the counter to make them more fluffy. Now cut a slice from the top of the medium potatoes. Cut the large ones in half lengthwise. Scoop out the insides and whip them with hot half-and-half and butter. Season with 2 tablespoons of the cheese and the salt and pepper. When fluffy, refill the potato skins. Sprinkle with the remaining cheese, and reheat at 400° for 5 to 8 minutes, until the cheese melts. *Serves 8.*

POTATO-CHEESE SOUFFLÉ

8 medium potatoes
¼ cup butter
1 cup hot milk
2 cups grated Cheddar cheese
1 teaspoon salt
¼ teaspoon pepper
2 eggs

Preheat oven to 350°. Boil the potatoes until tender. Peel and mash them with butter and milk. Add the cheese, salt, and pepper. Heat over a very low flame until the cheese is melted. Beat the eggs and fold in. Pour into a greased baking dish. Bake for about 35 minutes, until puffy and golden. *Serves 6.*

sauces

Sauces provide contrast, enhance and augment flavor; cheese sauces do even more!

CHEESE SAUCE

3 tablespoons butter
3 tablespoons flour
2 cups half-and-half
⅓ cup grated Cheddar
cheese

3 drops Tabasco or 1 tea-
spoon Worcestershire
sauce (optional)

Melt the butter and blend in the flour. Stir in the half-and-half. When smooth and thickened, stir in the cheese. Add the Tabasco or Worcestershire sauce if you wish. This is especially good over vegetables; try it with fish and egg dishes too. *Yield: about 2½ cups.*

HOT BLUE-CHEESE SAUCE

¼ cup olive oil
2 tablespoons lemon juice
½ teaspoon salt
¼ teaspoon pepper

¼ teaspoon sugar
4 ounces blue cheese,
crumbled

Blend the oil, lemon juice, salt, pepper, and sugar over low heat. Add the cheese and cook while stirring until smooth. This flavorful sauce is particularly good on vegetables such as spinach, kale, Swiss chard, and any drained cooked greens. *Yield: about 1 cup.*

BUTTER SAUCE WITH BLUE CHEESE

3 ounces blue cheese
¼ cup butter

2 tablespoons cream

Have the butter and cheese at room temperature. Smooth them together and blend in the cream. This is not only good on vegetables, but also as a spread or dip. *Yield: about ¾ cup.*

BUTTER SAUCE WITH PARMESAN CHEESE

½ cup grated Parmesan cheese

¼ cup butter, at room temperature
2 tablespoons cream

Blend the cheese and softened butter together thoroughly and stir in the cream. Good as a topping for pasta and as a dip, as well as over vegetables. *Yield: about ¾ cup.*

WHIPPED CREAM SAUCE WITH CHEESE

¾ cup grated Cheddar or Swiss cheese
2 teaspoons prepared mustard

1 teaspoon lemon juice
½ cup heavy cream, whipped

Fold the cheese, mustard, and lemon juice into the whipped cream. Spread on cooked asparagus, broccoli, spinach, or cauliflower and put under the broiler for about 1 minute, until the cheese is melted. *Yield: 1½ cups.*

salads

With cheese mixed in, sprinkled on, or poured over in a dressing, salads can be exciting.

CHEF'S SALAD I

Iceberg lettuce, leaf lettuce, Boston lettuce, escarole, watercress, young spinach, or Belgian endive (any combination) to cover the bottom of your salad bowl

2 tomatoes, peeled and cubed

1 cucumber, peeled and sliced paper thin

4 scallions, minced

½ pound tongue, cut into julienne strips

1 cup julienne strips of cooked chicken or turkey

½ pound Swiss cheese, cut into julienne strips

¾ cup *French dressing*

Tear up the greens. Put them into a large salad bowl; add the tomatoes, cucumber, and scallions. Scatter the strips of tongue, poultry, and cheese over the top. Pour the *French Dressing* over and toss at table. *Serves 8.*

CHEF'S SALAD II

2 heads salad greens, shredded (about 4 cups)
2 large tomatoes, peeled and
cut thin
2 cups diced celery
2 scallions, minced
½ pound ham, cut into strips
½ pound sharp Cheddar
cheese, cut in strips

1 can anchovies, drained and
cut in pieces
½ pound any cooked meat,
such as beef, pork,
lamb, or chicken, cut in
strips
1 cup *French* or *Lorenzo
Dressing*

Put the salad greens into a large salad bowl. Strew on the other ingredients. Pour on the dressing and toss at table. *Serves 8.*

SUNRISE SALAD

1 part smoked tongue (about
1 pound)
Lorenzo or *Wine French*
dressing

1 part Swiss cheese (about
1 pound)
1 part raw cabbage

Cut the tongue and cheese into julienne strips. Shred the cabbage. You need about the same amount of each ingredient. Combine everything in a salad bowl and mix. Top with *Lorenzo Dressing* or *Wine French Dressing*. Add the dressing slowly so you won't make the salad too wet. *Serves 4.*

SWISS SALAD

½ pound Swiss cheese
1 head lettuce
½ pound spinach or 1 bunch
　　watercress
¼ cup *Wine Mayonnaise*
1 tablespoon prepared
　　mustard

2 tablespoons olive oil
2 tablespoons red wine or
　　1 tablespoon red-wine
　　vinegar

Cut the cheese into julienne strips. Break up the greens and mix together with the cheese. Blend the *Mayonnaise* with mustard, oil, and wine or vinegar and pour over the greens. Toss. *Serves 6.*

LETTUCE STUFFED WITH
　　CHEESE

1 large head Boston lettuce
½ cup cottage cheese
2 ounces Roquefort cheese
2 tomatoes, peeled and diced

½ teaspoon Worcestershire
　　sauce
¼ teaspoon pepper

Wash the lettuce and gently separate the leaves without pulling the head completely apart. Mix the remaining ingredients. When well blended, stuff the mixture between the leaves. Chill. This is decorative. Cut it at the table. *Serves 6.*

TOMATOES STUFFED WITH CREAM CHEESE

6 large firm tomatoes	⅛ teaspoon basil
1 (8 oz.) package cream cheese or ½ pound Neufchâtel	¼ teaspoon sugar
	2 to 4 tablespoons *Mayonnaise*
½ teaspoon horseradish	Lettuce
¼ cup minced celery	

Peel the tomatoes and cut off the tops, making an opening large enough to permit the entry of a teaspoon. Scoop out the pulp and seeds and put into a bowl. Pour off excess liquid; stir in the cheese, horseradish, and celery and blend thoroughly. Season with the basil and sugar. Stir in as much *Mayonnaise* as you wish and adjust the seasoning. Refill the tomatoes and chill. Serve on lettuce. *Serves 6*.

TUNA-AND-CHEESE SALAD

2 (7 oz.) cans tuna	1 head lettuce, shredded
½ pound Cheddar cheese, diced	1 cup *Wine Mayonnaise*
	Leaf lettuce

Drain and flake the tuna and combine with cheese and lettuce. Stir in the *Wine Mayonnaise* gently. Taste for seasoning. Serve in a bowl lined with leaf lettuce. *Serves 6 to 8*.

LIME COTTAGE-CHEESE MOLD

1 (3 oz.) box lime gelatin
1 (3 oz.) box lemon gelatin
1½ cups boiling water
1 (8¼ oz.) can crushed pine-
     apple, drained
9 ounces (¾ of a 12-ounce
     carton) cottage cheese

½ cup *Mayonnaise*
½ cup evaporated milk
Pinch salt
½ cup chopped walnuts

Dissolve the gelatin in the boiling water. Chill. When cool, add the pineapple. Combine in a blender the cottage cheese, *Mayonnaise,* and evaporated milk, and buzz. Stir this cheese mixture into the gelatin mixture. Add a pinch of salt and the walnuts, and mix thoroughly. Pour into a one-quart mold or 8 custard cups, and chill until set. Unmold to serve. *Serves 8.*

PEACH AND NECTARINE SALAD

1 pound cottage cheese
2 tablespoons *Mayonnaise*
1 tablespoon lemon juice

1 tablespoon sugar
½ teaspoon salt
4 large peaches or nectarines

Combine the cheese with the *Mayonnaise,* lemon juice, sugar, and salt. Peel the peaches and slice each into 4 to 6 pieces. Nectarines should be sliced but not peeled. Pile the cheese mixture in the center of a cold platter or individual plates and stand the pieces of fruit around the cheese, pushing them in slightly so they stand up. If you use peaches, work fast and serve at once, as they darken. *Serves 4.*

PEARS STUFFED WITH CHEESE

1 pound cottage cheese
4 ounces blue cheese,
    softened
¼ cup minced parsley
1 tablespoon vinegar
¼ teaspoon pepper

½ cup heavy cream, whipped
4 pears (Bartlett, Comice, or
    Winter)
Lettuce
Mayonnaise (optional)

Blend the cheeses together. Add the parsley, vinegar, and pepper. Gently fold in the whipped cream. Peel, halve, and core the pears. Fill the cavities with the cheese mixture, mounding it. Serve on lettuce. Pass *Mayonnaise* thinned with a little orange juice, if you wish. *Serves 8*.

APPLE, PEAR, AND CHEESE SALAD

2 apples, peeled
2 pears, peeled
⅓ pound Swiss cheese

½ cup *Mayonnaise*, blended
    with 1 tablespoon lemon
    juice

Cut the apples, pears, and cheese in cubes. Mix at once with the *Mayonnaise*. *Serves 6*.

CHEESE BALLS FOR SALAD

1 (8 oz.) package cream
    cheese
Minced chives

Minced parsley
½ teaspoon salt
Paprika or chili powder

Have the cheese at room temperature. Stir in the chives, parsley, and salt. Form into small balls.

Sprinkle with paprika or chili powder. Refrigerate until firm. *Serves 8*.

CHEESE CURLS FOR SALAD

8 ounces Cheddar cheese

With a vegetable parer, slice thin strips of cold cheese and roll them. Chill and use as a garnish for salads.

CHEESE CROUTONS FOR SALAD OR SOUP I

4 slices stale bread   **Grated Swiss cheese**
Cold milk

Cut the crusts off the bread and cut it into small cubes. Dip them in cold milk and roll in the grated cheese. Bake at 450° for a few minutes until browned. *Yield: about 2 cups*.

CHEESE CROUTONS FOR SALAD OR SOUP II

4 thick slices bread   **Grated Parmesan cheese**
Melted butter

Brush the bread lightly with butter and cut into cubes. Fry cubes in butter until light brown on both sides. Put them in a bowl and sprinkle them with cheese. *Yield: about 2 cups*.

FRENCH DRESSING

⅓ cup wine vinegar
¾ teaspoon salt
¼ teaspoon pepper

¼ teaspoon dry mustard
1 cup olive oil

Mix the vinegar, salt, pepper and mustard thoroughly. Add the oil slowly while stirring. *Yield: 1⅓ cups.*

LORENZO DRESSING

1 bunch watercress
1 teaspoon sugar

¼ cup chili sauce
½ to ¾ cup *French dressing*

Cut up the watercress, discarding the tough stems. You need about a cupful. Add the sugar, chili sauce, and the *French Dressing*. The amount of dressing depends upon how thick you want the salad dressing. It should be quite thick with cress. *Yield: about 1½ cups.*

ROQUEFORT-TOMATO DRESSING FOR GREEN SALADS

4 ounces Roquefort or other
    blue cheese, softened
1 cup tomato juice
2 tablespoons lemon juice
1 tablespoon minced onion
    or scallions

2 tablespoons catchup
¼ teaspoon salt
¼ teaspoon pepper

Mash the cheese and blend in the rest of the ingredients. Beat with a rotary beater. *Yield: about 2 cups.*

BLUE-CHEESE SPREAD WITH BRANDY

4 ounces blue cheese
8 ounces cream cheese

3 ounces brandy

Have the cheeses at room temperature. Blend together, mashing the blue cheese with a fork. Stir in the brandy until the mixture is smooth. Good for stuffing celery or the leaves of Belgian endive. *Yield: about 2 cups.*

breads

For a change, add a cheese tang to your breads.

GARLIC CHEESE BREAD I

¼ pound butter
1 large or 2 small cloves
   garlic, crushed

Grated cheese, especially
   Parmesan
French bread

Cream the butter with the garlic and about 2 tablespoons of cheese. Slice the bread, being careful not to cut through the bottom crust. Make the slices about 1 inch thick. Spread them with the butter mixture. Brush the top with a little melted butter and sprinkle with more cheese. Heat in a 400° oven for 10 to 12 minutes. *Serves 4 to 6.*

GARLIC CHEESE BREAD II

1 loaf French bread
3 tablespoons butter, softened

1 clove garlic, crushed
½ cup grated Swiss cheese
¼ cup white wine

Preheat oven to 400°. Cut the bread into 1-inch slices, being careful not to cut through the bottom crust. Mix the softened butter with the garlic and cheese, add the wine, and stir until smooth. Spread the bread slices on both sides with this mixture. Heat in the oven for about 6 minutes, until hot. You may wrap the loaf in foil and heat for 10 minutes, if you wish. *Serves 4 to 6.*

TOASTED ENGLISH MUFFINS WITH CHEESE

4 English muffins
¼ cup soft butter

3 tablespoons grated cheese

Prick the muffins around the edge with a fork and pull them apart. You may cut them in half through the middle, which is quicker and easier; but tradition says,

"Pull apart with a fork." Butter the inside surfaces, sprinkle them with grated cheese, and toast in broiler, buttered sides up; do not turn. Watch them, they toast fast. *Serves 4.*

CHEESE BISCUITS

2 cups flour
1 tablespoon baking powder
1 teaspoon salt
½ cup grated sharp Cheddar cheese
⅓ cup shortening
¾ cup milk

Preheat oven to 450°. Sift the flour, baking powder, and salt together and stir in the cheese. Cut in the shortening until the dough has the consistency of coarse corn meal. Add the milk all at once and mix until smooth. Turn out on a floured board and knead briefly. Roll out ½-inch thick. Cut with a biscuit cutter or small glass. Bake on an ungreased cookie sheet for about 15 minutes. *Serves 4 to 6.*

CHEESE PATTY SHELLS

2 tablespoons butter
2 tablespoons flour
¼ cup cream
¼ cup grated Cheddar cheese
¼ teaspoon salt
Pinch cayenne pepper
1 egg white
6 packaged patty shells

Preheat oven to 325°. Melt the butter, blend in the flour, and stir in the cream and 2½ tablespoons of the grated cheese. Cook and stir over low heat until the cheese is melted. Season with ⅛ teaspoon salt and the cayenne. Remove from the heat. Whip the egg white with a pinch of salt until stiff. Gradually beat in the remaining cheese. Fill the patty shells with the cream-and-cheese mixture and top them with the cheese meringue. Bake for 10 minutes, until the meringue is golden on top. *Serves 6.*

desserts

Desserts made with cheese—what could be more delicious and more unusual?

CHEESE STRUDEL

2 cups flour
½ teaspoon salt
2 eggs plus 1 egg yolk
2 tablespoons cooking oil
½ cup lukewarm water
2 more tablespoons flour

1½ pounds pot cheese or
    cottage cheese
½ cup sugar
½ teaspoon vanilla
½ cup raisins (optional)
¼ cup melted butter
Confectioners' sugar

Sift the flour with the salt into a large bowl, make a well in the center, and put in 1 slightly beaten egg and the cooking oil. Stir while gradually adding the water to make a soft, rather sticky dough. Work the dough in the bowl until it comes away from the sides, turn out, and knead for about 15 minutes with little or no additional flour. Frequently slap the dough down hard on the board and work it until it is elastic and silky smooth. It must not stick to the hands or board. Form it into a ball, set it on a towel, and let it rest for an hour in a warm place, covered with a bowl which has been warmed in hot water. Warm your rolling pin. (This step is one of the keys to success.) While the dough is resting, cover the kitchen table—or a card table—with a cloth (a pressed piece of sheeting will do) and rub in about 2 tablespoons flour, brushing off any excess. Place the ball of dough in the center of the cloth and roll it with the warm rolling pin into a sheet ⅛-inch thick. Lift and turn it to prevent its sticking to the cloth. Take off your rings! Now flour your hands and with palms down under the dough stretch carefully from the center toward the outside. Don't raise your knuckles too high; make a fist and lift from the wrists only. Work carefully or you'll puncture the dough. (The holes can easily be repaired later, though.) Moving around the table, stretch the dough as thin as possible. Austrian cooks say the dough should be "as thin as paper." It should cover the table and hang slightly over the sides (about 30 x 40 inches). Trim off the edges, which will be a little thick. If you've made a hole, moisten the area around it with a little water and patch with a thin piece of dough from the trimmings. Let the dough rest and dry for 15 minutes while you prepare the filling.

Smooth the cheese and add the remaining egg and yolk, sugar, and vanilla. Add raisins if you wish. Mix well. Brush the entire surface of the strudel dough with the melted butter. Then spread the filling over the dough, leaving 3-inch margins on the ends and 2-inch margins on the sides. Fold the 3-inch end pieces over the filling and then the 2-inch margins, too. Lift the corners of the cloth and let the pastry roll up. Stop after each turn, patting the filled pastry to keep the bar shape even. Brush with more melted butter and slide the strudel onto a lightly buttered baking sheet, curving it into a U-shape. Bake at 375° for about 40 minutes, until golden brown. Sprinkle with confectioners' sugar and serve warm. *Serves 10 to 12.*

CHEESECAKE

Crust

1 (6 oz.) box zwieback
¼ cup sugar

¼ cup melted butter
½ teaspoon cinnamon

Filling

3 tablespoons flour
Pinch of salt
1½ cups plus 2 tablespoons
    sugar
18 ounces cream cheese, at
    room temperature

6 eggs, separated
1½ cups sour cream, at
    room temperature
1 teaspoon vanilla

Crush the zwieback and combine with sugar, melted butter, and cinnamon. Set aside ½ cup of this mixture and use the rest to cover the bottom and 1 to 2 inches up the side of a 9- or 10-inch springform pan that has been liberally buttered. Sift the flour, salt, and 1½ cups of the sugar together and cream it thoroughly with the cream cheese. Beat the egg yolks until thick and mix them with the cheese. Add the sour cream and vanilla. Mix again thoroughly. Beat the egg whites until stiff, gradually beating in the remaining sugar. Fold into the cheese mixture. Pour into the pan and sprinkle the remaining crumbs over the top. Bake at 325° for an hour. Turn oven off. Open the oven door an inch—prop it open with a spoon or a knife. Let the cake cool for another hour before taking it out of the oven. Do not remove it from the pan until completely cooled. If you do not cool it slowly in the oven as directed, the cake is likely to fall in the center, which spoils its appearance, although not its taste. This cake will keep fresh in the refrigerator for several days and is better the second day. *Serves 12.*

EASY CHEESECAKE

½ cup sugar
1 envelope gelatin
½ cup milk
1 egg, separated
1 pound small-curd cottage
cheese

1 tablespoon lemon juice
½ pint heavy cream,
whipped
Unbaked Crumb Crust

Dissolve the sugar and gelatin in the milk. Stir in the slightly beaten egg yolk and cook over low heat until thickened, stirring constantly. Smooth the cheese or press it through a coarse strainer. Stir in the milk mixture and the lemon juice. Chill, stirring several times, for half an hour. Beat the egg white until stiff and fold it in. Then fold in the whipped cream. Pour into the crust and chill again. *Serves 6.*

CHOCOLATE CHEESECAKE

1½ cups graham cracker
crumbs
¼ cup melted butter
1 cup sugar
3 eggs
1 (8 oz.) and 1 (3 oz.) package cream cheese,
softened

2 squares unsweetened
chocolate
1 teaspoon vanilla
1 cup sour cream

Mix the crumbs with the melted butter and 2 tablespoons of the sugar. Press onto the bottom and sides of a 9-inch springform pan. Beat the eggs. Add the remaining sugar gradually, beating until thick and smooth. Add the cheese a little at a time, beating steadily. Melt the chocolate in the top of a double boiler and blend it into the egg-cheese mixture. Add the vanilla and sour cream. Pour into the pan and bake at 350° for 30 to 40 minutes, until set. *Serves 10*.

CREAM CHEESE PIE

2 (8 oz.) packages cream cheese, at room temperature
¾ cup sugar
1 teaspoon lemon juice

½ teaspoon almond or vanilla flavoring
3 eggs
1 9-inch Unbaked Crumb Crust

Mix the softened cheese with the sugar, lemon juice, and flavoring. When thoroughly blended, add the eggs one at a time, mixing after each addition. Pour into the crust-lined pie pan and bake at 325° for about 30 minutes. Chill. *Serves 6*.

CHOCOLATE SOUFFLÉ

6 ounces cream cheese
⅓ cup milk
8 ounces semisweet chocolate, cut up; or 1 cup semisweet chocolate chips

5 eggs, separated
1 teaspoon vanilla
⅓ cup confectioners' or powdered sugar

Leave the cheese at room temperature for several hours. Mix it with the milk, using a rotary beater, and put it into a pot with the chocolate. Stir and heat until the chocolate melts. Preheat oven to 325°. Beat the egg yolks. Pour a little of the chocolate mixture into the eggs and then add all the egg mixture to the pot. Simmer and stir until slightly thickened. Remove from heat. Add the vanilla. Beat the egg whites until stiff and beat in the sugar a tablespoon at a time. Fold into the chocolate mixture and pour into an ungreased 1½-

quart soufflé dish or casserole. Place the dish in a pan of hot water and bake for about 50 minutes. Serve at once. *Serves 6 to 8.*

BAVARIAN CHEESE MOLD

2 envelopes gelatin
1 cup sugar
½ teaspoon salt
1 cup milk
2 eggs, separated

Juice and grated rind of
   1 lemon
3 cups small-curd cottage
   cheese
½ pint heavy cream

Combine the gelatin, sugar, salt and milk. Beat the egg yolks slightly and stir them into the gelatin mixture. Cook in a double boiler over low heat for 5 or 6 minutes until the gelatin and sugar are dissolved and the mixture coats a spoon. Add the lemon juice and rind to the cottage cheese and stir the cheese thoroughly into the gelatin mixture. Chill. Beat the egg whites until stiff and whip the cream. Gently fold the whites and cream together, and then fold into the cold milk mixture. Pour into a 2-quart mold or into 6 to 8 individual dishes. Chill. Unmold to serve. *Serves 6 to 8.*

CHEESE AND SHERRY MOLD

½ pound Camembert cheese
¼ cup sherry
½ pound unsalted butter (at
   room temperature)

Bread crumbs
2 pears
2 apples

Scrape the rind from the cheese. Pour the sherry over and smooth with the cheese. Let stand an hour or so and then put the mixture into the blender with the butter. Buzz at low speed for a few moments, spoon into a mold, top with crumbs, and chill. Unmold onto a serving plate and surround with wedges of pears and apples. *Serves 4 to 6.*

COEUR A LA CREME

1 (8 oz.) package cream cheese, at room temperature
1 cup small-curd cottage cheese
2 tablespoons heavy cream
1 tablespoon powdered or superfine sugar
Pinch salt
Mint or other greens (garnish)
Berries or *bar-le-duc* (currant) jelly

Beat the cheeses together until smooth, adding the cream slowly. Season with the sugar and salt. Line a heart-shaped basket or mold or other small basket or 9-inch springform mold with cheesecloth moistened with cold water. Fill with the cheese, pressing it gently. Fold the cheesecloth over the top and refrigerate overnight. Unmold onto a platter and decorate with a few sprigs of mint or other greens. Serve with berries or *bar-le-duc* jelly. You may substitute 1 cup sour cream for the cream and omit the cottage cheese. *Serves 4 to 6.*

COTTAGE-CHEESE RING WITH BERRIES

1 envelope gelatin
¼ cup water
2½ cups small-curd cottage cheese
Pinch salt
3 tablespoons sugar
1 cup sour cream
Strawberries, blackberries, blueberries, or raspberries
Powdered sugar

Soften the gelatin in the water and heat it to dissolve it. Mash the cottage cheese or press it through a sieve. Mix the cheese with the salt, sugar, sour cream, and gelatin. Spoon into an oiled 1-quart ring mold and chill. Turn out onto a cold platter and fill the center with lightly sugared berries. *Serves 4 to 6.*

RICOTTA DESSERT

1 (15 oz.) container ricotta cheese	2 to 3 tablespoons sugar
2 to 4 tablespoons milk	1 teaspoon cinnamon

Beat the ricotta with 2 tablespoons milk until smooth. You may need a little more milk to make it creamy but firm. Mix the sugar and cinnamon and stir in. Serve in parfait glasses. Or spoon cheese into the parfait glasses, layering the cinnamon-sugar between tablespoonfuls of the cheese. *Serves 4.*

CHEESE CROCK WITH SAUTERNE

1 pound Cheddar cheese, grated	2 tablespoons soft butter
¼ cup sour cream	¼ cup sauterne

Mash the cheese and combine it with the sour cream and butter. When well blended, stir in the sauterne. Put into a crock or bowl, cover tight, and refrigerate a couple of days before serving. *Serves 6.*

PREPARED CAMEMBERT

1 Camembert cheese, at
    room temperature
¼ pound softened unsalted
    butter

2 tablespoons heavy cream
Fine crumbs

    Scrape most of the crust off the cheese. It is easier
to do this with the dull side of a table knife. Mash the
cheese with the butter and cream. Pack it into an oiled
mold or shape it into a circle similar to its original
shape. Sprinkle it lightly with crumbs and chill for a
number of hours. Remove from refrigerator and let it
come to room temperature before serving. *Serves 6.*

CHEESE SAUCE WITH SOUR
CREAM

1 cup sour cream
4 ounces Cheddar cheese,
    shredded
1 tablespoon sugar

1 tablespoon lemon juice
1 teaspoon grated lemon
    rind

    Stir the sour cream, cheese, and sugar together in a
double boiler. Cook until cheese is melted. Remove
from heat and stir in the lemon juice and rind. Serve
cold over fruit. *Yield: about 2 cups.*

RHUBARB PIE

¼ cup cornstarch
3 tablespoons cold water
1½ cups sugar
4 cups rhubarb cut into
    1-inch pieces
9-inch Unbaked Pie Shell

2 eggs
1 (8 oz.) package cream
    cheese
Sour cream or whipped
    cream (optional)

Blend the cornstarch with the cold water and 1 cup of the sugar. Combine this with the rhubarb and stir and cook until soft and thickened. Pour into the pie shell and bake at 450° for 15 minutes. Meanwhile, beat the eggs and beat in the cheese and remaining sugar. When smooth, pour over the rhubarb and bake at 350° until puffy and lightly browned. Garnish with cream if you wish. *Serves 6.*

CHEESE-TOPPED APPLE PIE

9-inch apple pie   6 slices Cheddar-type cheese

Make or buy an apple pie. Place the slices of cheese over the top crust. Cover with a piece of foil. Do not press foil down; leave it loose. Heat at 400° until the cheese melts (about 10 minutes) and serve at once. *Serves 6.*

PASTRY FOR 9-INCH 2-CRUST PIE

2 cups flour   About 4 tablespoons ice
¾ teaspoon salt   water
⅔ cup shortening

To make good pie crust, the materials used should be very cold and the pie dough should be handled as little as possible. Sift the flour and salt together. Cut in the shortening with a pastry blender or 2 knives, until the mixture is in coarse particles a little larger than cornmeal. Sprinkle the water slowly, a tablespoon at a time, over different parts of the mixture, tossing lightly with a fork until the dough is moistened and will form a ball. Too much water makes the crust tough; too little, and it's crumbly. Wrap the ball of dough in waxed paper and chill it. Divide the chilled dough into 2 pieces and roll out into circles a little larger than the pie plate, ⅛ to ¼ inch thick. You can roll the dough on a lightly-floured pastry board or cloth, or between two pieces of waxed paper. Roll from the center and lift the rolling pin near the edge to keep the dough from splitting. If the edges split, pinch the cracks together. Ease the lower crust into the plate; don't stretch it. Pat out any air bubbles and trim the pastry evenly a half-inch beyond the plate edge. Gash the upper crust either before or after placing it over the filling, to let the steam out as the pie bakes. Seal the upper and lower crusts together around the edge with a little cold water. Roll the edges together or pinch or scallop the edges if you prefer. When the pie is ready to go into the oven, dot the crust with a bit of butter for extra flakiness. Or try glazing it by brushing it with a little water, milk, cream, or a mixture of an egg yolk beaten with a tablespoon water. You may also sprinkle the crust of fruit pies with a little sugar.

For a lattice top, roll half the pastry into a rectangle and cut strips of pastry ½-inch wide. Use a pastry wheel if you have one. Weave the strips across the top of the pie in crisscross fashion, moistening the ends, or braid them.

When making a berry pie, keep the juice from dripping out by building up the edge of the crust higher than usual. You can also try putting a small funnel into the center of the pie so that the juice will bubble into that.

Bake all pies at 450° to 475° for 10 minutes to set the crust before reducing the heat to about 350° for the balance of the baking time.

BAKED OR UNBAKED 9-INCH PIE SHELL

½ recipe *Pastry for 9-inch 2-Crust Pie*

Proceed as for a *2-Crust Pie,* rolling only one circle. Ease into the pie plate, letting the pastry hang over the rim. Pat out the air bubbles and trim the dough evenly a half-inch beyond the edge of the plate. Fold the overhang under, and crimp the edges with your fingers to make a neat rim.

For a baked shell, prick it *thoroughly* with a fork. Bake at 450° for 12 to 15 minutes. Another way to prevent the pie shell from buckling is to fit a piece of waxed paper into the shell and spread about 1½ cups of raw rice or beans over the paper. Remove the rice or beans and the paper after about 5 minutes of baking.

BAKED OR UNBAKED CRUMB CRUST

1½ cups graham-cracker or   ¼ cup sugar
    zwieback crumbs   ⅓ to ½ cup melted butter

Preheat oven to 350°. Mix the crumbs and sugar thoroughly with ⅓ cup of melted butter. Press the crumb mixture evenly on the bottom and sides of a buttered 9-inch pie plate. Bake for 5 minutes. Chill.

For an unbaked crust, use ½ cup butter and chill about an hour, until firm. *Yield: one 9-inch pie shell.*

CHEDDAR-CHEESE CRUST

Add 1 cup grated cheddar cheese when you cut in the shortening in the recipe for *Pastry for 9-Inch 2-Crust Pie.*

part two
wine

It is easy to guess how man discovered wine. Once upon a time, perhaps on a lazy late-summer day when the grapes were bursting ripe, he watched the antics of the wasps as they sipped and sipped again, and finally zigzagged off, staggering in their flight, blissfully tipsy. If the juice of the grape could make a wasp so happy, he would reason, it might contribute to lightening the lot of man. And so it proved.

But who invented cooking with wine? Was it a handmaiden too lazy to tote water from the well in which to simmer the stew? Was it a tipsy cook who spilled in some of his drink by mistake? Was it a wise philosopher who sagely reasoned that good things added to good things make good things better?

Whoever it was, she or he immediately discovered by nose that something good was brewing; and his teeth and palate soon confirmed that the new dish was transcendently tender and tasty.

From that day to this, we have known that cooking with wine does something very special. For one thing, its aroma perfumes the air like nothing else and tells the whole house that wine cookery is going on. It is the only way to make your kitchen smell like a fine French restaurant, and what better fragrance is there in the world than that?

Then again, a little wine in the dish adds distinction to the taste. Each kind of wine gives its own gift of flavor. Fortified wines like sherry and Marsala make desserts and sauces of very special deliciousness. Red wine tenderizes and flavors the lowliest cuts of beef, and white wine makes piquant the milder taste of chicken and fish. Rosé wine stands in for either. And think what wine can do to add a fillip to the return engagement of your planned leftovers.

Consider, too, that no other secret of Cordon-Bleu cookery costs so little. The price of the wine is but a small fraction of the total cost of the ingredients. Compare the cost of a cup of wine with what you pay for the pounds of beef it tenderizes. The bottle of wine you buy will flavor four or more delicious dishes. If corked and refrigerated, the wine can be kept on hand for a week or two—if you don't drink it first! Even if the last of it "turns" a little in the direction of vinegar, it will still be delicious in a salad dressing. All wine cookery demands some sugar—a pinch in white wine, a more generous pinch in red.

Speaking of pinching, do not pinch pennies on the wine. Pinch—if you must—on the costlier ingredients. Wine in your cooking is always well worth what it costs, for there is no more certain way to win plaudits and influence people at table.

Good wine, in a money-saving marinade, in a sauce, or in the cooking itself, improves every kind of meat and fish, and makes many a tasty salad dressing and delicious dessert.

What wine shall I buy to cook with, you ask? It needn't be an expensive vintage with a celebrated label. But remember, the water boils off, the alcohol boils off, what is left is the flavor. It is, therefore a mistake to cook with a wine that you don't like the taste of.

Don't be gulled into buying "cooking wine." It has been heavily salted so the kitchen wenches won't nip on it and get tipsy; and when it isn't salted, it is contaminated with vanilla.

But why trudge out to buy wine to cook with? If there is an inch left in your bottle of table wine, you can spike your food with it the next day. And if there isn't, perhaps when you open tonight's wine an hour before dinner, you can snitch a little to flavor the cooking.

Any way you work it, wine in the cooking enhances life, as the recipes to come will prove.

hors d'oeuvres

Wine does something for hors d'oeuvres, when you mix it in as well as when you drink it with.

PATÉ IN ASPIC

1 (10½ oz.) can consommé
1 envelope gelatin
¼ cup red wine, sherry, or port
¾ cup minced onion
1 small clove garlic, crushed
¼ cup butter
1 pound chicken livers

1 or 2 tablespoons water
3 hard-cooked eggs grated
2 tablespoons minced parsley
½ teaspoon oregano
1 teaspoon salt
½ teaspoon pepper

Mix the consommé with the gelatin and heat it to dissolve the gelatin. Add 2 tablespoons of the wine. Pour half the mixture into a wet, shallow bowl or dish, and chill. Sauté the onion and garlic in butter for 2 to 3 minutes. Add the livers and sauté gently for 10 minutes. Add a tablespoon or two of water, cover, and turn off heat. The livers should be cooked through gently but not browned. Mash them with a fork. If you want a really smooth paté, buzz at low speed in the blender with a few tablespoons of the wine-consommé mixture. But the fork routine gives more texture. Stir in the eggs, parsley, oregano, salt, pepper, and a little more wine-consommé. Spoon into the aspic. The aspic must be firmly set before you add the paté. Leave a little space around the edges, and pour in the remaining wine-consommé. If it has gotten too firm to pour, warm it very slightly. Refrigerate until the aspic is set. Run a knife around the edge and turn it out upside down on a plate. *Serves 8.*

CHICKEN-LIVER MOUSSE

1 pound chicken livers
½ cup chopped onion
¼ pound butter
½ pound liver sausage
½ cup Madeira or sweet
    sherry

1 (3 oz.) package cream
    cheese
¾ teaspoon salt
¼ teaspoon pepper

Cut up the livers and sauté them with the onion in the butter for 5 minutes. Add the liver sausage and cook 3 minutes more. Add the wine to the skillet; cook 5 minutes. Empty everything in the skillet into a blender and purée it, gradually adding the cream cheese, salt, and pepper, until a smooth paste is formed. Taste for seasoning, and pack into a bowl or crock. Cover and chill 4 hours. Serve in the crock. *Serves 8 to 10.*

MARINATED MUSHROOMS

1 pound small mushrooms
2 tablespoons soy sauce
¼ cup sweet sherry
3 tablespoons wine vinegar

2 tablespoons minced onion
1 tablespoon sugar
1 teaspoon salt
Pinch cloves

Pull out the stems from the mushrooms or cut them off flat. Place the caps in a jar. Mix the remaining ingredients and bring them to a boil. Pour them hot over the mushroom caps in the jar. Refrigerate for a day or two, covered. Be sure the mushrooms are covered with the liquid. *Serves 12 as a canapé.*

EGGS IN ASPIC

2 envelopes gelatin
3 cups chicken broth
1 cup dry white wine
2 tablespoons fresh tarragon
    leaves or 1 teaspoon
    dried tarragon

8 eggs, poached
Mayonnaise (optional)

Soften the gelatin in the broth, heat it until dissolved, and add the wine and tarragon. If using fresh tarragon, save 16 leaves and chop the rest. Chill until syrupy. Poach the eggs. Put 2 tarragon leaves across each other in each of 8 custard-size cups, pour in half the aspic, and chill. When firm, put a poached egg in each cup and fill with the remaining aspic. Chill until firm. If you've used the tarragon leaves, by all means turn out on plates; otherwise, you may leave the aspic in the cups. Serve with mayonnaise if you wish. *Serves 8 as an appetizer.*

CHEDDAR WITH PORT

½ cup port wine
½ pound Cheddar cheese,
    grated or shredded

2 tablespoons mayonnaise

Beat all ingredients together or buzz in a blender until smooth. Spoon mixture into a bowl or crock. Serve at room temperature. *Yield: about 2½ cups.*

BROILED GRAPEFRUIT

3 grapefruits
1 tablespoon sugar·

⅓ cup sherry
Brown sugar

Cut the grapefruit in half and loosen the sections. Sprinkle with a little sugar and dribble sherry over each half. Just before serving, sprinkle with brown sugar and put under the broiler until the sugar is lightly browned and the grapefruit hot. This will take only a few minutes. Watch so the sugar doesn't burn. *Serves 6.*

HONEYDEW WITH SAUTERNE

1 large honeydew melon

1 cup cold sauterne

Cut a plug from one end of the melon and remove the seeds through the opening with a long-handled spoon. Pour the sauterne into the melon, replace the plug, shake thoroughly, and refrigerate until ready to serve. Scoop out tablespoonfuls of the melon and serve in sherbet glasses with the wine from the melon poured over it. *Serves 6.*

soups

There's nothing like wine to cheer up a soup. One tablespoon of white wine per cup of clear soup makes a company treat. The same of red in a heavier soup passes the same miracle. Or try a touch of sherry in either. Or, best of all, choose a soup recipe that includes wine in the ingredients.

MADEIRA CONSOMMÉ

2 (10½ oz.) cans consommé
½ cup Madeira

Lemon slices

Heat the consommé, add the wine, reheat, but do not let boil, and serve at once with lemon slices floating on top. *Serves 4.*

MUSHROOM SOUP

1 cup dried mushrooms
1 cup water
2 tablespoons butter
1 tablespoon minced onion
2 tablespoons flour

3 cups beef broth or consommé
½ teaspoon salt
¼ teaspoon pepper
¼ cup dry sherry
Minced parsley (garnish)

Soak the dried mushrooms in the water for 2 hours. Drain, reserving the water, and chop. Melt the butter in a skillet. Sauté the onion 2 minutes. Then blend the flour into the butter. Add the broth while stirring constantly until thickened. Season with salt and pepper. Add the dried mushrooms and mushroom water. Simmer, covered, for 20 minutes. Just before serving, add the sherry. Serve sprinkled with parsley. *Serves 6.*

ITALIAN MUSHROOM SOUP WITH MARSALA

¼ cup butter
¼ cup flour
1 quart hot milk
1 teaspoon salt
¼ teaspoon pepper

1 pound mushrooms, chopped
1 clove garlic, minced
3 tablespoons minced parsley
¼ to ½ cup Marsala

Melt 2 tablespoons of the butter, blend in the flour, and when smooth, pour in the hot milk while stirring. Add the salt and pepper and simmer, covered, for 10 minutes. Meanwhile, sauté the mushrooms and garlic in the remaining butter for 2 to 3 minutes. Add the parsley and Marsala. Stir well and pour into the milk mixture. Reheat and reseason to taste. If the soup is too thick, add a little more wine or milk. *Serves 6.*

EASY BOULA

1 (10¾ oz.) can pea soup
1 (10½ oz.) can turtle soup

3 tablespoons Madeira or sweet sherry
¼ cup cream, whipped

Heat the soups together and add Madeira. Put into individual ovenproof soup bowls. Top with cream and put under broiler for 1 minute to brown. *Serves 4.*

TOMATO SOUP WITH WINE

1 cup dry white wine
3 cups beef broth
4 cups tomato juice
½ cup sliced onion
2 sprigs parsley
2 stalks celery
1 teaspoon sugar

¼ teaspoon freshly ground
    black pepper
2 cloves
¼ cup dry sherry
Lemon slices
Paprika

Combine the wine, broth, tomato juice, onion slices, parsley, celery, sugar, pepper, and cloves in a saucepan. Bring to a boil, and cook over low heat 20 minutes. Strain, return broth to saucepan. Mix in the sherry and taste for seasoning. Heat and serve in bouillon cups, with a slice of lemon sprinkled with paprika floating on top. Serve this soup chilled if you wish. *Serves 8.*

JELLIED TOMATO-SHERRY SOUP

3 envelopes gelatin
4 cups tomato juice
½ teaspoon salt
1 teaspoon sugar
1 teaspoon Worcestershire
    sauce

1 tablespoon lemon juice
⅓ cup sherry
Minced parsley or chives
Lemon slices or wedges

Soften the gelatin in ½ cup of the tomato juice, add the remaining juice, and heat and stir until the gelatin is dissolved. Remove from heat and add the seasonings and sherry. Chill until set, 3 or 4 hours. Spoon into cups, garnish with parsley and/or chives, and serve with a piece of lemon. *Serves 4 to 5.*

TOMATO-CLAM SOUP

4 tablespoons butter
1½ cups chopped onion
2 cups chopped tomatoes
1 clove garlic, minced
2 cups dry white wine

4 cups bottled clam juice
¼ teaspoon white pepper
2 (8 oz.) cans minced clams
2 tablespoons minced parsley

Melt the butter in a saucepan; sauté the chopped onion 10 minutes. Add the tomatoes and garlic; cook over low heat 5 minutes. Mix in the wine, clam juice, and pepper. Buzz the clams in a blender. Add to the soup. Cook, covered, over medium heat 20 minutes. Stir in the parsley. *Serves 8.*

CLAM SOUP WITH WHITE WINE

2 (8 oz.) cans minced clams
¾ cup white wine
¼ teaspoon white pepper
2 cups bottled clam juice

2 egg yolks
¼ cup heavy cream
1 tablespoon butter

Buzz the clams, the wine, pepper, and bottled clam juice in a blender. Bring to a boil, and cook over low heat 3 minutes. Beat the egg yolks and cream together in a bowl; gradually add some of the hot soup, stirring steadily. Return this mixture to the balance of the soup and heat and stir, but do not let boil. Add the butter just before serving. *Serves 6.*

FISH SOUP

3 tablespoons butter	½ teaspoon black pepper
3 tablespoons olive oil	½ teaspoon rosemary
4 celery ribs, chopped	6 cups hot water
4 onions, chopped	2 pounds cod fillets or
2 carrots, chopped	whiting
4 ripe tomatoes, peeled and	2 pounds of any other inex-
diced or 1 small can	pensive white fish
Italian plum tomatoes	1 cup white wine
1½ teaspoons salt	

In a large pot heat the butter and oil; sauté the celery, onions, and carrots in it until soft. Stir in the tomatoes and season with salt, pepper, and rosemary. Simmer, covered, for 15 minutes. Add the hot water, bring to a boil, reduce heat, and simmer, covered, for 20 minutes more. Add the fish fillets. Simmer, uncovered, for 20 minutes. Remove the fish while still firm, and keep warm. Strain remainder through sieve, forcing fish, vegetables, and stock through, or buzz in a blender. Bring to a boil. Add the wine and fish and reheat. *Serves 10.*

ITALIAN FISH SOUP

3 pounds assorted white fish	1½ cups chopped onion
⅓ cup olive oil	1 clove garlic, minced
1½ teaspoons salt	2 tablespoons tomato paste
½ teaspoon black pepper	3 cups dry white wine
1 teaspoon finely chopped	1 cup boiling water
bay leaf	

Cut the fish into serving-size pieces. Heat the oil in a heavy saucepan; brown the fish in it lightly. Season with the salt, pepper, and bay leaf; cook uncovered over low heat for 5 minutes, turning the pieces once. Carefully remove the fish and keep warm. In the remaining oil sauté the onion for 5 minutes. Mix in the garlic, tomato paste, and wine; add the boiling water. Cook covered over low heat 20 minutes. Return the fish to pan and simmer uncovered 10 minutes longer. *Serves 8.*

SHRIMP SOUP

2 tablespoons olive oil
2 tablespoons butter
2 carrots, chopped
2 celery ribs, chopped
½ teaspoon basil
1 tablespoon chopped parsley
2 white onions, chopped

1½ teaspoons salt
½ teaspoon black pepper
½ pound fresh shrimps in their shells
6 cups chicken broth
½ cup dry white wine
½ cup Marsala

In a large pot heat the oil and butter and sauté the carrots, celery, basil, parsley, onions, salt, and pepper for 10 minutes. Add the shrimps in their shells and the chicken broth; simmer, covered, for 20 minutes. Uncover and add the white wine and Marsala. Turn off the heat. Remove the shrimps, peel, cut each one into 3 or 4 pieces, and return to pot. Reheat. *Serves 6 to 8.*

SWEET GERMAN FRUIT SOUP

1 pound plums
1 pound peaches
½ pound cherries
4 cups water
4 cups white wine

1 cup sugar
½ teaspoon cinnamon
1 tablespoon cornstarch
4 tablespoons sweet sherry
Whipped cream

Wash the fruit. Cut the plums and peaches in half and discard the pits. Pit the cherries. Combine the fruits with the water, white wine, sugar, and cinnamon. Bring to a boil, and cook over low heat 30 minutes, or until the fruits are very soft. Purée them in a blender, or force through a sieve. Return them to the saucepan. Mix the cornstarch with the sherry and stir it into the soup. Cook over low heat, stirring steadily until the soup is thickened. Add more sugar or cinnamon to taste. Chill. Serve with a spoonful of whipped cream on top. *Serves 8.*

GERMAN WINE SOUP

3 eggs, separated
4 cups dry white wine
1 cup broth
¼ teaspoon cinnamon
⅛ teaspoon ground cloves
1 teaspoon sugar
½ teaspoon salt

Bring the wine, broth, cinnamon, cloves, sugar, and salt to a boil. Beat the egg yolks in a bowl. Gradually add a little of the hot wine mixture, stirring steadily. Return this to the wine mixture. Heat, but do not let boil. While heating, beat the egg whites until stiff. Fold them in. *Serves 4 to 6.*

CHILLED PEACH-WINE SOUP

4 (10½ oz.) cans peach
   nectar
½ tablespoon grated lemon
   rind
2 tablespoons instant tapioca
1½ cups white wine
4 egg yolks, beaten
4 ripe peaches
1 tablespoon Cointreau,
   Curaçao, or Grand
   Marnier (optional)

Heat the nectar with the lemon rind. Stir in the tapioca and cook for 5 minutes. Stir the wine into the beaten egg yolks; then stir mixture into the hot nectar. Chill. Just before serving, peel, pit, and dice the peaches. Pour the liqueur over them, and stir into the soup. *Serves 6.*

fish and shellfish

Fish is happy swimming in wine.

TROUT IN WINE ASPIC

2 cups dry white wine
¾ cup water
1½ teaspoons salt
¼ teaspoon white pepper
1 tablespoon minced parsley

¼ teaspoon tarragon or dill
4 brook trout
1 tablespoon gelatin
3 tablespoons dry sherry

In a skillet, combine the wine, water, salt, pepper, parsley, and tarragon or dill. Bring to a boil, and cook over low heat 10 minutes. Arrange the trout in the skillet. Bring to a boil again, cover, and simmer 15 minutes. Carefully transfer the trout to a serving dish. Soften the gelatin in the sherry, then stir into the hot stock until dissolved. Pour over the fish and chill until set. *Serves 4.*

FISH FILLETS IN WINE

2½ pounds fillets of sole,   1 tablespoon lemon juice
    flounder, or any white-   1 teaspoon salt
    flesh fish   ¼ teaspoon pepper
1½ cups white wine   2 tablespoons butter

Put the fillets in a pan large enough to hold them
flat without overlapping. Combine the remaining ingredients except the butter and pour over the fish.
Bring to a boil, reduce the heat, cover, and simmer
until the fish flakes with a fork, about 10 minutes. Remove the fish to a warm platter. Reduce the wine liquid
to about half, add the butter, and serve with or over
the fish. *Serves 6.*

POACHED SMALL FISH OR STEAKS

1 cup dry white wine   *Wine Cream Sauce, Sauterne*
3 cups water   *Butter Sauce,* or *Wine*
2 teaspoons lemon juice   *Hollandaise*
½ teaspoon salt
6 small fish such as trout or
    3 pounds fish steaks
    such as halibut

Pour the wine, water, and lemon juice into a deep
skillet or pan. Add the salt and bring to a boil. Put in
the fish and simmer them, covered, for about 15 minutes, depending upon the size of the pieces of fish;
steaks cook faster than whole fish. Remove them carefully to heated plates or a platter, using a perforated
spoon or turner. Serve with the sauce of your choice.
Serves 6.

POACHED FILLETS OF SOLE

3 cups water
1 onion, sliced
1 clove garlic, slivered
1 bay leaf
1 slice lemon
1 stalk celery
Celery leaves
Parsley sprigs
⅛ teaspoon thyme

1 teaspoon salt
Peppercorns
½ cup white wine
Fish heads and scraps
3 pounds fillets of sole
Flour seasoned with salt and
    pepper
4 tablespoons butter

Bring 3 cups water to a boil with the onion, garlic, bay leaf, lemon, celery stalk and leaves, parsley, thyme, salt, peppercorns, and ¼ cup of the wine. Add the fish heads and scraps and simmer, uncovered, for half an hour. Remove from heat and strain. Dust the fillets lightly with seasoned flour. Place them in a buttered shallow pan or casserole and dot them with butter. Add 1½ cups fish stock. Simmer 5 minutes, add the remaining wine, and simmer 5 minutes more. Serve in the casserole; or put the fish on a platter, bring the sauce in the casserole to a boil for 1 minute, and pour over the fish. *Serves 8.*

FISH FILLETS SAUTÉED IN WHITE WINE

4 pounds fillets of red snap-
    per, sole, or flounder
½ teaspoon salt
¼ teaspoon pepper
¼ cup butter

¾ cup white wine
Lemon juice
2 tablespoons flour or 2 egg
    yolks, beaten

Sprinkle the fillets with salt and pepper and sauté in butter for about 7 minutes. Turn, pour half the wine over the browned side of the fish, and cook 5 to 6 minutes more. Put onto a warm platter with the last browned side up and sprinkle with a few drops of lemon juice. Thicken the sauce left in the pan by stirring the flour or beaten egg yolks with the other half of wine. Stir and heat until smooth, and pour over the fish. *Serves 8 to 10.*

FISH CASSEROLE

4 slices bacon
6 fillets sole (2½ lbs.)
2 teaspoons salt
½ teaspoon pepper
1½ cups minced onions
1 cup grated carrots
½ pound mushrooms sliced
3 tablespoons minced
   parsley
½ cup peeled, chopped
   tomatoes
½ teaspoon dill
2 cups dry white wine
3 tablespoons butter

Fry the bacon until it begins to brown; drain and crumble it. Season the fillets with salt and pepper. Spread the bacon on the bottom of a shallow, greased casserole. Mix together the onion, carrots, mushrooms, parsley, tomatoes, and dill. Spread half this mixture over the bacon. Arrange the fish over the vegetables and cover them with the remaining vegetable mixture. Add the wine, and dot with the butter. Bake in a 350° oven for 45 minutes. *Serves 6.*

FISH STEW IN WHITE WINE

4 pounds assorted fresh-
   water fish
2 slices bacon
Water
¼ cup butter
2 tablespoons olive oil
3 tablespoons flour
4 cups white wine
1 clove garlic, minced
2 teaspoons salt
¼ teaspoon freshly ground
   black pepper
1 bay leaf, finely crushed
2 tablespoons minced parsley
Sautéed or toasted French
   bread slices

Cut the fish into serving-size pieces. Cover the bacon with water; bring to a boil, then drain and chop the bacon. Heat the butter and oil in a casserole; brown the chopped bacon in it. Stir in the flour over low heat until browned. Gradually add the wine, stirring constantly. Mix in the garlic, salt, pepper, bay leaf, and parsley. Cover and continue to cook over low heat 30 minutes. Add the fish and cook, covered, for 20 minutes. Arrange sautéed bread slices on top around the edges of the casserole. Serve in soup plates. *Serves 8.*

BURGUNDY FISH STEW

Follow the directions for *Fish Stew in White Wine,* substituting red Burgundy for half the white wine.

MACKEREL STEW

3 pounds mackerel, filleted	¼ teaspoon pepper
½ cup chopped onion	1 tablespoon sugar
2 tablespoons olive oil	¾ cup red wine
4 ounces tomato paste	1 tablespoon wine vinegar
¼ cup water	Rice
1 teaspoon salt	

Cut the fish into bite-size pieces. Sauté the onion in the oil until it is transparent but not brown. Add the tomato paste mixed with ¼ cup water, the salt, pepper, sugar, wine, and vinegar, and the fish. Simmer, covered, for 20 minutes. If you've cooked this in a pyrex dish or casserole, serve it in the dish; otherwise, transfer it to a bowl. Serve rice on the side. *Serves 6.*

SEA BASS POACHED IN FOIL

1 sea bass, head and tail on (about 3 lbs.)	Leaves of lettuce
1½ teaspoons salt	1 cup white wine
¼ teaspoon pepper	Butter

Have a large piece of heavy foil ready. Rub the fish inside and out with salt and pepper. Place the fish on lettuce leaves on the foil and pour the wine over. Dot with butter. Fold the foil over the fish, envelope-fashion, to seal completely. Bake at 450° for 30 minutes. Reduce heat to 350° and bake another 30 minutes. Serve the fish in its foil on a warm platter and unwrap it at the table; or slide it off the foil with the juices. *Serves 4.*

BAKED SALMON STEAKS

4 slices salmon, 1 inch thick (about 2 lbs.)	¼ cup grated carrot
2 teaspoons salt	3 tablespoons butter
½ teaspoon black pepper	2 tablespoons flour
¾ cup chopped onion	2 cups dry white wine
	1 bay leaf

Preheat oven to 400°. If the salmon slices are large, cut each in half through the bone. Season with the salt and pepper. In a large skillet, sauté the onion and carrot in the butter for 5 minutes. Blend in the flour; gradually add the wine, stirring steadily. Pour the sauce into a baking dish and arrange the fish in it. Add the bay leaf. Cover the dish with aluminum foil. Bake for 30 minutes, until the fish flakes easily when tested with a fork. *Serves 4 to 6.*

FISH KEBABS

2 pounds firm fish, such as swordfish	½ cup white wine
Juice of 1 lemon	½ teaspoon salt
	Bay leaves

Cut the fish into 1- to 1½-inch cubes. Marinate for several hours in a mixture of the lemon juice, wine, and salt, with 1 crushed bay leaf. Thread on skewers with a piece of bay leaf between some of the pieces of fish. Broil 5 minutes, turn and broil 5 minutes more. Baste frequently with the marinade. *Serves 6.*

SCALLOPS WITH WHITE WINE

2 shallots or 4 scallions, minced	1½ pounds bay or sea scallops
¼ cup dry white wine	¼ pound small shrimps, shelled
2 tablespoons white vinegar	¼ cup minced parsley
¼ cup fish broth, or bottled clam broth	¼ pound butter
	1 cup heavy cream

Put the shallots or scallions into the wine, white vinegar, and broth and simmer for 2 minutes. If you use sea scallops, cut each into 4 pieces. If you can get tiny shrimps, leave them whole; otherwise, cut them once through the center. Add the scallops and shrimps to the liquid and poach until tender, about 5 minutes. Add the butter and cream. (If you have small oven-proof shells, fill and brown under the broiler for 3 to 4 minutes.) *Serves 4.*

SCALLOPS AND SHRIMPS WITH WHITE WINE

1 pound scallops
1 pound small shrimps, peeled
1 cup water
1 cup dry white wine
2 tablespoons minced scallions or onion

3 tablespoons butter
½ pound mushrooms, sliced
1 tablespoon flour
1 teaspoon salt
2 tablespoons half-and-half

If the scallops are large sea ones, cut them in half or in quarters; if bay scallops, leave them whole. Unless the shrimps are quite small, cut once through the center the long way; if very large, cut them once more, making quarters. Cut the scallops raw; the shrimps are easier to cut after they've been cooked. Simmer the scallops and peeled shrimps gently in the water mixed with the white wine for 5 minutes. Meanwhile, sauté the scallions or onion in butter for 3 or 4 minutes, but do not let brown. Add the mushrooms and cook 3 minutes more. Stir in the flour and salt and 1 cup of liquid from the fish. Add the half-and-half and the scallops and shrimps. Heat and adjust seasoning to taste. If the sauce is too thick, add more liquid from the fish; if too thin, add a little more flour made into paste with the liquid. *Serves 6.*

SHRIMPS DE JONGHE

1 clove garlic, crushed
¼ cup minced parsley
⅔ cup dry sherry
1 cup butter, melted
½ cup bread crumbs

1 pound cooked shrimps,
    peeled
¼ cup any grated cheese
    (optional)

Preheat oven to 350°. Add the garlic, parsley and sherry to the melted butter. Mix and toss in the bread crumbs. Put the shrimps, whole if small, cut lengthwise if large, into a shallow baking dish. Cover with the crumb mixture and top with cheese, if you wish. Bake until heated through and the crumbs are brown. *Serves 2 to 4.*

SHRIMP SOUFFLÉ

1 cup water
1 cup white wine
1½ teaspoons salt
1 onion, cut up
1 pound raw shrimps, shelled
    and deveined

3 tablespoons butter
3 tablespoons flour
½ cup heavy cream
½ teaspoon dry mustard
4 eggs, separated

Preheat oven to 375°. Combine the water, ½ cup of the wine, 1 teaspoon salt, and the onion in a saucepan; bring to a boil. Add the shrimps, reduce heat, and cook over low heat 5 minutes. Drain. Strain the shrimp liquid, reserving half a cup. Chop the shrimps coarsely. Melt the butter, blend in the flour, and gradually mix in the ½ cup shrimp liquid, the remaining wine, and the cream, stirring steadily. Blend in the mustard and remaining salt. Simmer 5 minutes. Beat the egg yolks in a bowl; stir some of the hot sauce into the yolks and return yolks to the pan, stirring constantly. Stir in the shrimps. Cool 10 minutes. Beat the egg whites until stiff; fold into the shrimp mixture. Turn into a buttered 1½-quart soufflé dish; bake 35 minutes, or until browned and set. Serve immediately. *Serves 4 to 6.*

SHRIMPS NEWBURG

4 tablespoons butter	4 egg yolks
1 pound shelled cooked shrimp	1 cup half-and-half
	2 tablespoons brandy
½ teaspoon salt	¼ cup dry sherry
½ teaspoon sugar	Nutmeg
½ teaspoon Cayenne pepper	

Melt the butter in a double boiler. Add the salt, sugar, and pepper, and sauté the shrimps for 3 minutes. Stir the egg yolks into the half-and-half and add to the shrimps. Continue to cook, stirring constantly, until mixture thickens. Stir in the brandy and sherry. Sprinkle with nutmeg. *Serves 4.*

SCALLOPS NEWBURG

Proceed as for *Shrimp Newburg,* substituting 1 pound of raw scallops for the shrimps, and cooking them in the butter 10 minutes, or until done.

poultry

Fowl is fine when cooked with wine.

CHICKEN BREASTS IN SHERRY

6 chicken breasts (skinned   1 teaspoon salt
    and boned)   ¼ teaspoon pepper
½ cup dry sherry   ¼ cup butter

Place the chicken breasts in a low bowl and cover
with the sherry. Chill for several hours or overnight.
Turn 2 or 3 times to insure each breast's being covered
with the sherry. Remove from the sherry, sprinkle with
salt and pepper, and sauté in butter. When browned,
turn and brown the other side. Pour the sherry over,
and simmer covered about 20 minutes more, until
tender. Place the chicken on a warm platter and pour
the liquid over it. *Serves 6.*

BROILED CHICKEN WITH
SHERRY

2 (2½ to 3 lb.) frying   ¼ teaspoon pepper
    chickens   ¼ cup flour
½ cup melted butter   ¼ cup dry sherry
1 teaspoon salt

Split and quarter the chickens. Brush with melted
butter and sprinkle with a mixture of the salt, pepper,

and flour. Broil for 25 minutes, skin side up. Brush with sherry, turn, add more butter and the remaining sherry, and broil 20 minutes more. Serve skin side up and pour any juices over. *Serves 6 to 8.*

ROAST CHICKEN WITH WHITE WINE OR VERMOUTH

1 (4 to 5 lb.) chicken
1 teaspoon salt
¼ teaspoon pepper
½ teaspoon dry rosemary or 2 teaspoons minced fresh

¼ cup soft butter
¾ cup white wine or vermouth
2 to 3 tablespoons flour
1 cup chicken broth

Preheat oven to 450°. Rub the chicken inside and out with salt, pepper, and rosemary. Put 2 tablespoons butter inside the chicken. Rub the remaining butter on the chicken. Roast for 15 minutes, baste with wine, reduce heat to 350°, and roast for half an hour, covered loosely with foil. Remove the foil, baste with wine, and cook 15 minutes more. If the chicken is not as brown as you want, cook at 450° for the last few minutes. Thicken juices with flour and add the chicken broth to make gravy. *Serves 5.*

CHICKEN IN CHAMPAGNE

2 (3 to 3½ lbs.) chickens
2 teaspoons salt
¼ teaspoon pepper
¼ cup butter
3 tablespoons minced onion
2 tablespoons minced carrot

2 tablespoons minced parsley
¼ cup minced mushrooms
½ cup water
1 cup champagne
½ cup heavy cream

Rub the chickens with salt and pepper. Put them in a casserole with the butter and brown them lightly. Add the onion, carrot, parsley, and mushrooms. Stir and brown for a few minutes. Add ½ cup water and then ½ cup champagne. Cover and simmer until chickens are tender, about 45 minutes. Baste several times and turn them. Remove the chickens to a warm platter. Boil juices for 2 minutes, then add cream and remaining champagne and heat. Pour a little of the sauce over the chickens and serve the rest in a bowl. *Serves 8.*

CHICKEN IN WINE AND CREAM SAUCE

2 (3 lbs.) frying chickens, cut up	1½ cups white wine
2 teaspoons salt	¼ cup brandy warmed
¼ cup butter	3 egg yolks
2 cloves garlic, split	1½ cups cream

Rub the pieces of chicken with 1 teaspoon salt and brown them in butter with the garlic. After 15 minutes remove the garlic and add the white wine and brandy. Bring to a boil, ignite, shake the pan, and stir until the brandy has finished burning. Cover and simmer until the chicken is tender, about 15 minutes. Place the chicken on a hot platter. Beat the egg yolks with the cream. Add to the pan. Simmer gently until thickened, and pour the sauce over the chicken. *Serves 8.*

BELGIAN CHICKEN

6 cups chicken broth
3 slices lemon
2 cups dry white wine
3 tablespoons melted butter

2 (2½ to 3 lbs.) quartered
    chickens
½ cup dry bread crumbs

Combine the broth, lemon slices, wine, and butter in a casserole. Bring to a boil and add the chicken. Simmer covered for 30 to 40 minutes, or until chicken is tender. Stir in the bread crumbs, adjust the seasoning, and serve directly from the casserole in bowls. *Serves 6.*

CHICKEN IN WINE

2 (2½ to 3 lbs.) frying
    chickens, cut up
6 tablespoons butter
Salt
1 cup diced salt pork
3 scallions, minced
1 (16 oz.) can small white
    onions, drained

1 clove garlic, crushed
3 medium carrots, sliced
6 tablespoons brandy
1½ tablespoons flour
2 cups red wine
1 cup sliced mushrooms
½ teaspoon sugar

Sauté the chicken pieces in the butter over medium heat until golden brown. Remove the pieces as they brown to a large casserole, salting them lightly. In the same pan, sauté the salt pork, scallions, onion, garlic and carrots. When lightly browned, discard the garlic and, with a slotted spoon, remove the rest to the top of the chicken in the casserole. In the same pan, heat the brandy, ignite it, and shake over heat until burning ceases. Sprinkle in the flour, and stir over low heat 2 or 3 minutes. Stir in the wine and bring to a boil, scraping up the glaze. Add the mushrooms and sugar. Salt to taste. Add more sugar if the wine needs it. Pour the sauce over the chicken and vegetables in the casserole. Cover and bake at 350° for about an hour. *Serves 6.*

CHICKEN CASSEROLE WITH WHITE WINE

2 (2½ to 3 lbs.) chickens, cut up
¼ cup butter
6 scallions or 1 medium onion, minced

2 cups dry white wine
1 teaspoon salt
¼ teaspoon pepper
2 tablespoons flour

Sauté the chicken in 3 tablespoons butter until browned. Put into a casserole. Sauté the scallions or onion in the pan the chicken was browned in, adding remaining butter. Pour in the wine, scrape the pan, and pour the wine-onion mixture over the chicken. Season with salt and pepper. Bake, covered, at 350° for about an hour. Thicken juices with a little flour-and-water paste. *Serves 6.*

CHICKEN AND VEGETABLES WITH VERMOUTH

1 (10¾ oz.) can mushroom
   soup
⅔ cup dry vermouth
1 tablespoon minced parsley
½ teaspoon crushed rose-
   mary
1 cup celery, cut in small
   pieces
2 (3 lbs.) chickens, cut up
1 tablespoon salt
1 teaspoon pepper
3 tablespoons butter or salad
   oil or a combination of
   both

½ cup water
1 (16 oz.) can very small
   onions
2 packages (10 oz.) frozen
   peas and carrots,
   thawed
1 package (10 oz.) frozen
   French-cut green beans,
   thawed
1 package (10 oz.) frozen
   hash-browned potatoes,
   thawed, or 1 (16 oz.)
   can small potatoes

Pour the mushroom soup into a large Dutch oven or casserole; stir in the vermouth. Add the parsley, rosemary, and celery. Sauté the chicken pieces, which have been sprinkled with salt and pepper, in butter or oil until light brown. Put them into casserole. Boil the water in the skillet; add it to the casserole. Simmer, covered, on top of the stove until fairly tender, about 40 minutes. Add the onions, thoroughly drained, peas and carrots, green beans, and potatoes. If you use canned potatoes, drain and brown them lightly in 1 tablespoon butter or oil before adding. Simmer, covered, for 15 minutes; correct the seasoning. Although this gravy is supposed to be thin, it can be thickened with flour-and-water paste if you wish. *Serves 10.*

CORNISH GAME HENS

6 game hens (about ¾ lb.
    each) or 3 large ones
    cut in half
2 teaspoons salt
½ teaspoon pepper

¼ teaspoon poultry season-
    ing
⅓ cup soft butter
2 tablespoons flour
1 cup white wine
3 strips bacon (optional)

Thaw the birds. Rub inside and out with a mixture of salt, pepper, and poultry seasoning. Blend 3 tablespoons butter with the flour and rub all over the birds. Roast in a 350° oven for about 40 minutes. Baste frequently with the wine combined with the remaining butter. Put the bacon slices over the breasts for the last 20 minutes of cooking, if you wish. *Serves 6.*

DUCK WITH ORANGE AND
    PORT WINE

2 (5 lbs.) ducks
2 cups water
1 onion
¼ teaspoon thyme
½ bay leaf

3 teaspoons salt
½ teaspoon pepper
3 oranges
1 cup port wine

Preheat oven to 450°. Place the giblets, necks, and wing tips in a pot with 2 cups water, the onion, thyme, bay leaf, and 1 teaspoon salt. Simmer, covered, for 45 minutes. Meanwhile, rub the ducks with 1 teaspoon salt and ¼ teaspoon pepper each. Cut 1 orange into 8 pieces (skin and all), and put 4 in each duck. Place in the oven for 20 minutes. While the ducks are roasting, slice 1 orange very thin. Grate the rind of the third orange with a coarse grater to make slivers and then squeeze the juice. Prick the breasts of the ducks to release the fat and pour off excess fat. Reduce heat to 350°; pour the port wine and orange juice over the ducks. Baste every 10 minutes, turning the birds to insure even browning. They should not require more than an hour more of cooking unless they are old or large birds. When done, place them on a warm platter. Garnish with orange slices. Skim the fat from the pan juices, add the orange peel and 1 cup of strained broth from the giblets. Thicken with a flour-and-water paste. *Serves 6 to 8.*

ROAST GOOSE OR DUCK WITH WHITE WINE

1 (10 lbs.) goose or 2 (5 lbs.) ducks
1 teaspoon salt
¼ teaspoon pepper

¾ cup prepared stuffing
1 to 2 cups white wine
Butter
Flour

Preheat the oven to 425°. Dust the bird or birds with salt and pepper and fill with the dressing of your choice. Put on a rack and roast uncovered for an hour for a goose, half an hour for ducks. Prick the goose several times to allow the fat to run out. Ladle the fat from the pan. Reduce heat to 350° and baste with the wine every few minutes. If the ducks are dry, add a little melted butter when basting. Cook a total of about 30 minutes to the pound. If the breasts are not brown enough, turn the oven back to 450° for the last 15 minutes of cooking. To make gravy, pour off all juices and put into the freezer for a few minutes to bring the fat to the top. Remove as much fat as possible. Add flour to thicken. Then return the juices and remaining wine to the pan the bird(s) were roasted in and heat. *Serves 6 to 8.*

ARGENTINIAN DUCKS

Follow the instructions for *Roast Goose or Ducks with White Wine,* but make sauce by stirring flour into juices and adding the juice and grated rind of 1 orange, and ½ cup more white wine. When thickened, add 1 ounce of brandy.

STUFFED TURKEY

3 cups dry red wine
2½ cups chopped onion
2 cloves garlic, minced
4 teaspoons salt
1 teaspoon freshly ground
 black pepper
1 bay leaf
12-pound turkey
⅓ cup olive oil

¾ cup chopped green
 peppers
2 cups chopped almonds
1¼ cups seedless raisins
½ teaspoon poultry seasoning
2 cups diced bread
Soft butter

In a bowl, combine the wine, 1 cup of the chopped onion, the garlic, 2 teaspoons of salt, the pepper, and the bay leaf. Marinate the turkey in this mixture in the refrigerator overnight. Turn a few times. Heat the oil in a skillet; sauté the green peppers and remaining onion 5 minutes. Season with the remaining salt and mix in the almonds, raisins, poultry seasoning, and bread. Taste for seasoning. Preheat oven to 350°.

Drain the turkey, stuff it, and close the openings with skewers or thread. Place it in a roasting pan breast side up, and brush with soft butter; roast for 3½ to 4 hours, pouring the marinade over it after 1 hour. Baste frequently. If the breast gets too brown, place a piece of foil loosely over it. *Serves 10.*

BLANQUETTE OF TURKEY

1 pound cooked ground
    turkey meat
2 slices white bread mois-
    tened with milk or water
½ teaspoon Worcestershire
    sauce
½ teaspoon nutmeg
½ teaspoon salt
1 egg
½ cup white wine
½ cup water

2 tablespoons flour
2 tablespoons butter
1½ cups milk or half-and-
    half
½ teaspoon nutmeg
½ teaspoon Worcestershire
    sauce
2 teaspoons instant chicken
    broth
½ teaspoon sugar
Noodles

Mix turkey, bread, Worcestershire sauce, nutmeg, salt and egg, lightly but thoroughly. The mixture will be light. Bring the wine and water to a simmer and drop the turkey mixture by rounded spoonfuls into it. Cover and poach 12 minutes over low heat. Do not over-cook.

To make the sauce, lightly brown the flour in the butter over medium heat, stirring constantly. Gradually add the milk or half-and-half and bring slowly to a boil, stirring constantly. Season with nutmeg, Worcestershire sauce, instant chicken broth, and sugar. Drain the liquid from the poached turkey balls into the sauce and blend in. Correct the seasoning, bring to a boil, and pour over the turkey. Serve with noodles. *Serves 4.*

CHICKEN LIVERS WITH RED WINE

2 onions, sliced thin
¼ cup olive oil
1½ pounds chicken livers
¼ cup flour

1 teaspoon salt
¼ teaspoon pepper
Pinch oregano
⅓ to ½ cup red wine

Sauté the onions in oil until softened. Cut the livers in half. Sprinkle the livers with flour, salt, pepper, and oregano. Sauté them with the onions for 3 or 4 minutes, turning frequently. Add the wine and bring to a boil. *Serves 4.*

meats

When it comes to meat, wine is the big money-saver. There is something about wine that tenderizes as it perfumes the most economical cuts and turns them into gourmet treats. Marinated, basted, or simmered with wine, beef and other meats become something to brag about.

STEAK WITH WHITE WINE

6 (6 oz.) fillets of beef or 6
    small shell or other
    boneless steaks
2 tablespoons olive oil
½ teaspoon salt

1 teaspoon freshly ground
    pepper
½ cup dry white wine
¼ cup butter
Minced parsley

Rub the steaks on both sides with oil, salt, and pepper. Put into a very hot skillet and cook 1 minute only on each side. Add the wine, reduce heat, and simmer, covered, for 2 to 4 minutes. Remove the beef to a hot platter. Turn heat to high, add the butter, and stir. Add the parsley and pour the foaming butter over the steaks. *Serves 6.*

STEAK IN RED WINE

Proceed as for *Steak with White Wine,* substituting ½ cup red wine for the white.

STEAK DIANE

4 (8 oz.) club steaks, cut ¼ inch thick or 4 (6 oz.) fillets cut ½ inch thick
2 teaspoons prepared French mustard
2 tablespoons bottled steak sauce
¼ cup butter
2 tablespoons brandy
⅓ cup dry sherry
1 tablespoon chopped chives or green onions

Trim the steaks, then rub with a mixture of the mustard and the steak sauce. Cook the steaks over high heat in 2 tablespoons of the butter for 2 to 3 minutes on each side. Warm the brandy, pour it over the steaks, and ignite. Add the sherry, chives, and remaining butter. Transfer the steaks to a hot serving dish. Reheat the sauce and pour it over the steaks. *Serves 4.*

STEAK WITH BLACK PEPPER

2 tablespoons coarsely
    ground peppercorns
2 pounds club or shell
    steaks, cut 1 inch thick
1 tablespoon olive oil or
    butter
2 tablespoons butter

1 tablespoon chopped shal-
    lots or onion
1 cup dry red wine
1 teaspoon prepared mustard
1 teaspoon Worcestershire
    sauce
2 tablespoons warm brandy
    (optional)

With the palm of your hand, press the crushed
peppercorns well into both sides of the steaks. Heat the
oil or 1 tablespoon butter in a skillet; quickly brown
the steaks in it on both sides. Melt 1 tablespoon of
butter in another skillet; sauté the chopped shallots or
onion 2 minutes. Add the steaks, and cook 2 minutes
on each side. Remove the steaks to a heated platter
and keep hot. Add the wine to the shallots; cook over
high heat until it is reduced to ¼ the original quantity.
Remove from the heat and stir in the mustard, Worcestershire sauce, and the remaining butter, broken into
small pieces. If you wish add warm brandy and ignite.
Reheat the sauce and pour over the steaks. *Serves 2
to 4.*

SWISS STEAK WITH WINE

¼ cup flour
1½ teaspoons salt
¼ teaspoon pepper
4 pounds round steak, cut
    into serving pieces
4 tablespoons butter

1 cup chopped onion
1 clove garlic, minced
1 cup red wine
½ teaspoon marjoram
1 bay leaf
1½ teaspoons sugar

Mix together the flour, salt, and pepper. Dip the steak in the mixture, then pound the mixture in. Brown the steak in the butter in a heavy skillet, turning once. Add the onion and garlic and cook 5 minutes more. Add the wine, marjoram, bay leaf, and sugar. Simmer, covered, for about 2 hours, basting and turning the meat frequently. Discard the bay leaf. *Serves 8.*

STEAK-AND-KIDNEY PIE

4 to 6 veal kidneys or 2 beef kidneys
2 pounds top round steak
¼ cup flour
2 tablespoons oil or butter
1 cup thinly sliced onion
½ pound mushrooms, sliced
2 teaspoons salt
½ teaspoon pepper
½ teaspoon thyme
1 tablespoon tomato paste
1 cup red wine
½ recipe for *Pastry for 9-inch 2-Crust Pie*

Cut the kidneys in half or in bite-size pieces, removing the hard core. Cut the steak into 1-inch cubes. Toss the meat and kidneys with the flour. Heat the oil or butter in a skillet; brown the meat and kidneys in it. In a buttered 2-quart casserole, arrange layers of the sautéed meats, onion, and mushrooms. Mix together the salt, pepper, thyme, tomato paste, and wine; pour into the casserole. Bake, covered, in a 350° oven about 2 hours. Carefully place the pastry over the meat mixture and press the edges down with a fork. Make a few gashes in the top. Increase the heat to 400° and bake 25 minutes more, or until the pastry is browned. *Serves 6.*

BEEF A LA MODE

1 (4 lb.) boneless piece beef chuck or rump
2 teaspoons salt
1 cracked veal knuckle
3 carrots, sliced
2 onions, sliced
5 cups water
1 cup white wine
2 cloves
6 peppercorns, crushed

1 bouquet garni (4 sprigs parsley, 2 sprigs fresh or 1 teaspoon dried thyme, and 2 bay leaves)
16 small white onions, lightly browned in butter
8 carrots, cut in half
2 or 3 tablespoons flour

Have the butcher lard the beef and tie a piece of fat around it. Preheat oven to 375°. Rub meat with 1 teaspoon salt and sear it in a greased skillet until brown. Place it in a Dutch oven or other heavy pot with a lid; add the veal knuckle. Brown the sliced carrots and onions in the same skillet and rinse it into the pot or Dutch oven with 1 cup of the water. Add 4 more cups of water and the white wine, cloves, peppercorns, 1 teaspoon salt, and the bouquet garni. The liquid should cover the meat. Bring to a boil, cover, and put in the oven for 3½ hours. This can also be cooked on top of the stove, keeping it just below the boiling point. Remove the meat to a side dish and strain the broth. Return the meat and strained broth to the pot. Add the small browned onions and the halved carrots. Cook about another half hour, until the vegetables are done. Place the meat on a platter, remove the fat that was tied around it, and surround it with the vegetables. For thick gravy, add 2 to 3 tablespoons flour made into a paste with a little cold water, and simmer a few minutes. Spoon some of the sauce over the meat and serve the rest separately. *Serves 8.*

BEEF BOURGUIGNON

4 pounds trimmed lean
    sirloin or round steak
6 slices bacon or ¼ pound
    salt pork, diced
2 cloves garlic, crushed
2 pounds mushrooms, sliced
2 bay leaves, crushed

2 tablespoons chopped
    parsley
1 teaspoon salt
1 teaspoon thyme
⅛ teaspoon pepper
½ cup butter
½ cup flour
1 bottle red Burgundy

Cut the beef with the grain into strips about ½ inch by 4 inches. Cut the bacon or pork into small pieces and fry them in a Dutch oven. Remove the pork or bacon, and sauté the beef strips in the drippings. Stir frequently but remove as soon as evenly browned. You will have to brown a portion at a time. Add the garlic and mushrooms. Season with the bay leaves, parsley, salt, thyme, and pepper. Put the bacon or salt pork back in the pot. Remove from heat. In another pan make a roux by melting the butter and stirring in the flour. Cook, stirring constantly, until the flour turns light tan. Add the wine, stir and cook until slightly thickened. Add this to the beef and mushrooms. Cover and simmer until the beef is tender, about 1½ hours. Add more salt if needed. This may be made ahead and reheated in a casserole just before serving. *Serves 8 to 10.*

BEEF STEW

2 tablespoons butter
2 tablespoons flour
1 cup beef broth or bouillon
1 cup red wine
1 teaspoon salt
½ teaspoon freshly ground
    black pepper
12 small white onions,
    peeled

6 potatoes, peeled and
    quartered
2 tablespoons minced
    parsley
¼ teaspoon thyme
2½ lbs. stewing beef, cut
    in ½-inch cubes

Melt the butter in a saucepan; blend in the flour until browned. Gradually mix in the broth and wine, stirring steadily. Add the salt and pepper, onions, potatoes, parsley, and thyme and cook over low heat 5 minutes. Add the beef. Simmer, covered, for 30-45 minutes, or until beef is tender. *Serves 6.*

BEEF STEW WITH FRUIT

2 tablespoons olive oil
2 tablespoons butter
2 pounds beef, cut into
    1-inch cubes
1½ cups chopped onion
1½ cups dry white wine
1 tablespoon tomato paste
1 bay leaf
2 teaspoons salt
½ teaspoon pepper

½ teaspoon thyme
1 cup beef broth or bouillon
2 pears, peeled and cubed
2 peaches, peeled and
    sliced
2 apples, peeled and cubed
3 tablespoons seedless
    raisins
Rice

Heat the oil and butter in a heavy casserole; brown the beef in it. Remove the meat and brown the onion in the fat remaining in the pan. Return the meat, and stir in the wine, tomato paste, bay leaf, salt, pepper, thyme, and broth. Bring to a boil, cover, and cook over low heat 1 hour. Carefully mix in the pears, peaches, apples, and raisins. Cook, covered, 15 minutes. Taste for seasoning, and serve with rice. *Serves 8.*

BEEF STEW WITH BLACK OLIVES

3 pounds beef rump, cut
    into 1-inch cubes
2 tablespoons olive oil
2 tablespoons butter
2 tablespoons brandy
    (optional)
1 cup red wine
½ teaspoon salt

¼ teaspoon pepper
¼ teaspoon sugar
1 tablespoon minced parsley
½ teaspoon thyme
1 clove garlic, crushed
½ pound pitted black olives,
    bulk or canned
Rice or noodles

Brown the beef in a mixture of the oil and butter. If you are using the brandy, warm it, pour it over the meat, and ignite. Shake the pan as you work. Add the wine, salt, pepper, sugar, parsley, thyme, and garlic. Simmer, covered, for 1½ to 2 hours, until the beef is tender. You may need to add a little more wine or water to keep the meat moist. Add the olives, reheat, and adjust the seasoning to taste. Serve with rice or noodles. *Serves 6 to 8.*

POT ROAST

½ pound salt pork, diced
1 (3½ to 4 lbs.) piece of
    beef top round, rump,
    brisket, or chuck
2 large onions, sliced
3 carrots, sliced
3 tomatoes, peeled and
    sliced

2 cloves garlic, minced
1 bay leaf
1 tablespoon minced parsley
1 teaspoon thyme
½ cup red wine
½ teaspoon salt
¼ teaspoon pepper
Flour (optional)

Brown the salt pork in a heavy pot like a Dutch oven, remove pieces, and reserve. Brown the beef on all sides in the drippings. Add the vegetables, herbs, wine, salt, and pepper. Cover and simmer about 2 hours, or cook in a 350° oven for 3 hours until the meat is tender. Remove the meat to a warm platter and thicken the juices with a little flour-and-water paste if you wish. Pour a little over the roast and serve the rest on the side. This dish is good with rice, noodles, or mashed potatoes. *Serves 6 to 8.*

SHORT RIBS BURGUNDY

Short ribs of beef (about
    4 to 5 lbs.), cut into
    serving-size pieces
3 tablespoons flour
3 tablespoons bacon fat
1 cup chopped onions
2 teaspoons salt
½ teaspoon pepper

¼ teaspoon marjoram
½ cup water
1 cup red Burgundy wine
1 cup beef broth
8 medium potatoes, peeled
    and cut in half
8 small carrots
16 small white onions

Roll the short ribs of beef in 2 tablespoons of the flour. Brown them slowly on all sides in the bacon fat. Add the chopped onions, salt, pepper, marjoram, ½ cup water, and the Burgundy. Cover and simmer for an hour. Skim off the excess fat and add the broth. Simmer, covered, for another half hour. Add the potatoes, carrots, and the small white onions. Cover and simmer until the vegetables are tender, about another half hour. Thicken with remaining flour and adjust the seasoning. *Serves 8.*

MEAT LOAF WITH WINE

1½ pounds ground beef	¼ teaspoon freshly ground
¼ pound minced prosciutto,	pepper
Smithfield ham, or	¼ cup grated Parmesan
Canadian bacon	cheese
¼ cup seasoned bread	1 cup bouillon or consommé
crumbs	½ cup red wine
½ teaspoon salt	Bay leaves

Mix the beef and ham together thoroughly. Stir in the bread crumbs, salt, pepper, and cheese. Moisten with the broth and wine, using it all. The meat will be quite soft and hard to handle. Line a flat pan with bay leaves. Form the meat into a loaf and place on top of the bay leaves. Bake at 350° for about 45 minutes. *Serves 4 to 6.*

BEEF-AND-VEAL PATTIES IN WINE

2 pounds ground beef	1 teaspoon salt
1 pound ground veal	¼ teaspoon pepper
4 eggs	1½ cups red wine
1 large onion, chopped fine	¾ pound mushrooms
¼ cup minced parsley	Flour (optional)

Mix the meats with the eggs, onion, parsley, salt, and pepper. Divide into 8 patties. Pour half the wine into an ovenproof dish or casserole. Put in the patties and bake at 350° for 15 minutes. If the mushrooms are small, leave them whole; otherwise, cut them in halves or quarters through stem and cap. Add to the dish together with the remaining wine, and cook 15 minutes more. Remove the patties and thicken the juices with a little flour-and-water paste, if you wish. *Serves 8.*

RED-WINE MEATBALLS

2 pounds ground beef
2 tablespoons minced
    onions or shallots
1 teaspoon salt

¼ teaspoon pepper
2 tablespoons butter
½ cup Burgundy or other
    red wine

Mix the meat with onions or shallots. Season with salt and pepper, and form into balls. Brown quickly on all sides in very hot butter. Add the wine, cover tight, and simmer for 4 minutes for rare or 6 minutes for medium. Pour any juices over the meat. *Serves 6.*

TONGUE IN WHITE WINE

4 to 6 medium carrots,
    sliced in rounds
2 medium onions, sliced
    thin
2 tablespoons rendered
    bacon fat
3 cloves

11 peppercorns
1 teaspoon salt
½ teaspoon pepper
1 fresh beef tongue, about
    3 lbs.
1 to 2 cups white wine
Rice or noodles

Sauté the carrots and onions in the bacon fat, adding the cloves, peppercorns, salt, and pepper. Put the tongue in the pot over half the vegetables and pile the other half on top. Pour over the wine. Marinate 24 hours, turning several times. (The greasy sautéed vegetables are Escoffier's trick for keeping the top moist, as wine to cover would be too much wine.) Be sure in turning the tongue to renew the vegetable cover. After the 24 hours, cook in the same pot, simmering 3 to 4 hours, till very tender. Skin the tongue and return to marinade. At this point the tongue may be sliced in a casserole, and the marinade poured over. Serve with rice or noodles. *Serves 4 to 6.*

ROAST VENISON

6 pound saddle or leg of
venison
¼ pound salt pork
(optional)
1 onion, chopped
1 carrot, chopped
3 tablespoons olive oil

1 tablespoon tarragon
1 tablespoon salt
¼ teaspoon pepper
1 cup red or dry white wine
Sugar
Flour

Have the venison larded or buy ¼ pound of salt pork. Venison is a dry meat and needs to be lubricated. Sauté the onion and carrot for 5 minutes in the oil with tarragon, salt, and pepper. Add the wine; red wine is richer, but white wine is more delicate and so does not hide the venison flavor. If you use red wine add a generous pinch of sugar. Place the meat in this marinade for 12 to 48 hours, turning it from time to time. When ready to cook, place the meat in an open pan. If it is not larded, cover with the salt pork. Add a little of the marinade and roast at 400°, for about 20 minutes. Reduce heat to 350°, and roast for about 40 minutes more. Twelve minutes to the pound will be medium, 10 minutes rare. Baste every 15 minutes with the marinade and juices. Remove the roast and thicken the gravy with a little flour-and-water paste. *Serves 8.*

SWISS VEAL STEAKS

2 pounds veal from the shoulder or leg	½ cup butter (1 stick)
1 teaspoon salt	1 tablespoon minced onion or scallions
¼ teaspoon pepper	½ cup dry white wine
Pinch sugar	1 cup beef broth or bouillon
1 teaspoon paprika	1 cup dry sherry
¼ cup flour	

Cut the veal into narrow strips about 2 inches long. Mix the seasonings with 2 teaspoons of the flour and toss the veal in this mixture. Sauté them in 2 tablespoons of the butter while stirring. Remove from heat. Sauté the onion in 2 more tablespoons of butter for 2 minutes, until transparent. Add it to the veal and add the wine. Simmer for 5 minutes. Melt the remaining ¼ cup butter and blend in the remaining flour. When smooth, add the beef broth slowly while stirring, and then the sherry. Boil 1 minute and add to the veal. Reheat. *Serves 6.*

VEAL CHOPS WITH WHITE WINE

6 to 8 thick veal chops	2 cups finely grated onions
1 teaspoon salt	¼ pound salami, diced
3 tablespoons butter	2 cups white wine

Sprinkle the chops with salt and brown them in very hot butter for 1 minute on each side in an iron skillet or Dutch oven. Mix the onion and salami and spread it over the chops. Pour the wine over and simmer, covered, for 5 minutes. Put into a 350° oven and bake for an hour. *Serves 6.*

VEAL STEW WITH VERMOUTH

3 pounds veal from a boned
    loin end or a lean
    shoulder
1 teaspoon salt
¼ teaspoon pepper
1 tablespoon olive oil
1 tablespoon butter

1 large onion, sliced
1 cup water
½ cup dry vermouth
2 tomatoes, peeled and
    quartered
Flour

Cut the veal into 1-inch pieces. Sprinkle them with salt and pepper and sauté for a few minutes in the oil and butter. Add the onion and sauté 2 minutes more. Pour in the water and wine, add the tomatoes, and simmer, covered, for about an hour, until the veal is tender. Thicken the juices with a little flour-and-water paste. *Serves 6 to 8.*

SALTIMBOCCA

2 pounds veal scaloppine,
    about 12 slices
6 tablespoons butter

12 slices prosciutto
1 tablespoon flour
¼ cup white wine

Brown the veal in 4 tablespoons very hot butter; turn and brown the other side. Put a slice of prosciutto on each veal slice and pin it in place with a toothpick. Cook about 1 minute more and remove to a warm platter. Add 2 tablespoons butter and the flour to the pan. When blended, add the wine while stirring. Pour this sauce over the veal. *Serves 6.*

OSSO BUCCO

3 to 4 pounds veal knuckle or shank	1½ teaspoons salt
Flour	¼ teaspoon pepper
¾ cup oil	½ cup beef or chicken broth
¾ cup chopped onion	1 cup dry white wine
¾ cup chopped celery	1 (8 oz.) can tomato sauce
¾ cup chopped carrots	1 tablespoon grated lemon peel
2 cloves garlic, crushed	Rice

Have the meat and bone cut into 3-inch pieces. Roll in flour and brown on all sides in hot oil. Add all of the chopped vegetables, garlic, salt, and pepper. Cover and simmer 10 minutes. Add the broth, wine, tomato sauce, and peel, and simmer, covered, for 1 to 1½ hours, until the meat is very tender. Serve the sauce over the meat. If you want it thicker, add a little flour and water paste. Serve with rice or saffron rice. *Serves 6.*

LAMB STEAKS WITH WINE

2 pounds lamb steaks or shoulder chops	2 tablespoons olive oil
1 teaspoon salt	2 onions, sliced thin
¼ teaspoon pepper	1 to 2 tablespoons flour
2 tablespoons butter	1 cup white wine

Season the lamb with salt and pepper and brown in
the butter and oil for 1 minute on each side. Add the
onions and sauté for about 10 minutes, turning the lamb
occasionally and stirring the onions. Blend the flour
into the wine, pour it over the meat, and simmer 3 or 4
minutes more. *Serves 4 to 6.*

RAGOUT OF LAMB

3 to 4 pounds breast and
    shoulder of lamb
¼ cup flour
1 teaspoon salt
¼ teaspoon pepper
2 tablespoons butter
2 cups broth

6 to 8 carrots, cut into
    2-inch lengths
2 medium onions, sliced
½ cup red wine
½ pound mushrooms
    (optional)

Have the lamb cut into bite-size pieces. Dust them
with a mixture of the flour, salt, and pepper. Brown in
butter for a few minutes. Add the broth and simmer,
covered, for an hour. Add the carrots, the onions, and
wine. Simmer, covered, for another hour. Add the
mushrooms if you wish and cook 15 minutes more.
The juices will not need thickening. *Serves 6.*

LAMB STEW WITH RED WINE

3 pounds boneless lamb,
    cut in 1½-inch cubes
¼ cup flour
2 teaspoons salt
¼ teaspoon pepper
½ teaspoon thyme
3 tablespoons butter

3 tablespoons warmed
    cognac (optional)
3 cups red wine
2 cups chopped onions
2 cups diced carrots
1 bay leaf

Roll the lamb in a mixture of the flour, salt, pepper, and thyme. Brown in butter. Pour the warmed cognac over the meat if you wish and ignite it. When the flames die, add the wine, onion, carrots, and bay leaf. Bake, covered, at 350° for 2 hours. Skim off the fat and discard the bay leaf. If gravy is too thin, thicken it with a little flour-and-water paste. *Serves 8.*

LAMB WITH VERMOUTH

3 to 3½ lbs. boneless
    shoulder of lamb, cut
    in 1-inch cubes
2 tablespoons butter
2 teaspoons salt
¼ teaspoon pepper
½ cup dry vermouth
1 package frozen artichoke
    hearts, cooked and
    drained, or 1 (8½ oz.)
    can, drained

4 eggs
½ cup grated Parmesan
    cheese
2 tablespoons minced
    parsley

Brown the lamb in the butter in a casserole or deep skillet. Season it with salt and pepper. Add the wine; boil for 5 minutes. Cover, and bake at 350° for an hour. Add the artichokes and a little boiling water if necessary. Bake 10 minutes longer. Beat the eggs, cheese, and parsley together, and pour over the lamb. Bake uncovered for 10 minutes more. *Serves 6 to 8.*

NEAR EAST MEAT AND VEGETABLE CASSEROLE

1 pound lean lamb	1 medium eggplant, peeled
1½ pounds lean pork	¼ cup minced parsley
1 pound lean beef	¼ cup chopped celery
6 large tomatoes, peeled and sliced	1½ teaspoons salt
1 teaspoon sugar	¼ teaspoon pepper
1 pound zucchini or summer squash	¼ cup olive oil
	¾ cup rice
1 pound onions, peeled	1 cup red wine
	⅓ cup dry grated cheese

Preheat oven to 350°. Cut the meats into small cubes. Sprinkle the tomatoes with the sugar. Cut the other vegetables into cubes and combine them with the parsley, celery, salt, and pepper. Put a third of the tomatoes on the bottom of a casserole, add half the mixed vegetables and half the meats, half the rice, and half the oil. Repeat. Top with the remaining third of tomatoes. Then pour the wine and the last of the oil over. Bake, covered, for about an hour and a half. Top with the cheese for the last 20 minutes of baking time. *Serves 8*.

WINE MARINADE FOR KEBABS

1 cup red or white wine, vermouth, or sherry	½ cup corn or peanut oil
¼ cup lemon juice	1 onion or 1 clove garlic, chopped

Use red wine for lamb, beef, game, or kidneys; white or dry vermouth for chicken, fish, or shellfish; sherry for chicken livers or veal. Use the onion for beef, lamb, or veal; the garlic for lamb, kidneys, or chicken livers, if you wish. Marinate for several hours. *Yield: about 2 cups.*

KEBABS

2 pounds lean boneless lamb, cut in 1-inch cubes
Wine Marinade for Kebabs
1 onion cut in rounds, or 1 pound small white onions, parboiled
1 green pepper, parboiled and cut into 1-inch squares
½ pound medium-size mushrooms
½ pound young zucchini, cut in rounds
Melted butter

Marinate the lamb cubes for several hours. Thread on 6 good-size skewers, alternating with any 2, 3, or 4 of the suggested vegetables. Brush the kebabs with the marinade and melted butter. Broil for 3 to 4 minutes, turn, and broil 3 minutes more, basting the kebabs after you turn them. *Serves 6.*

KEBAB VARIATIONS

Lamb with onions and green pepper and/or eggplant
Beef with mushrooms and green tomatoes
Veal with zucchini and mushrooms
Kidneys with bacon and onions
Chicken livers with mushrooms and bacon
Chicken with mushrooms and cherry tomatoes

Shrimp with mushrooms
Fish with bay leaves, onions, or green pepper
Satay: ground beef with ginger and pineapple slivers

ROAST PORK WITH WINE

1 (4 to 5 lbs.) loin of pork
1 teaspoon salt
1 to 2 tablespoons prepared
    mustard

1½ cups white wine
2 tablespoons flour

Rub the roast with salt and spread it with mustard.
Pour the wine over it and let it stand for several hours.
Roast it at 450° for 15 minutes, reduce to 350°, and
roast for 2½ hours more, until tender. Baste with
wine frequently. Skim off fat. Thicken juices with flour-
and-water paste. *Serves 6.*

PORK TENDERLOIN WITH
VERMOUTH

2½ pounds pork tenderloin
1 teaspoon salt
¼ teaspoon pepper
1 clove garlic, crushed

½ teaspoon dry mustard
1 cup dry vermouth
1 to 2 tablespoons sweet
    vermouth

Place the meat in a bowl and rub it with a mixture
of the salt, pepper, garlic, and mustard. Pour the wine
over and let stand for several hours in the refrigerator.
Turn frequently to see that all the meat is covered. Bake
at 400° for 15 minutes, reduce to 350°, and bake half
an hour more. Add a little more wine if needed to
baste the pork several times. *Serves 6.*

SWEET AND SOUR PORK

1 medium onion, sliced
1 small green pepper, sliced
1 cucumber, sliced
1 large carrot, cut into
    rounds
2 cups water
2 to 2½ lbs. lean pork, cut
    into 1-inch cubes

¼ cup cornstarch
2 tablespoons soy sauce
1 teaspoon sugar
3 cups sake or sweet sherry
Oil for frying
1½ cups pineapple chunks
Rice

Sauce

¼ cup sugar
¼ cup vinegar
3 tablespoons cornstarch

½ cup pineapple juice
2 tablespoons sake or
    sweet sherry

Simmer the vegetables in 1 cup water for 10 minutes. Simmer the pork in remaining water for 10 minutes. Make a batter by blending the cornstarch with soy sauce, sugar, and sake or sherry. Drain the pork and dip into the batter. Heat the oil and fry the pork until brown and crisp. Drain on paper toweling. Make the sauce by combining all of the sauce ingredients in a saucepan. Simmer, while stirring, until thickened. Add the fried pork, the drained vegetables, and the chunks of pineapple to the sauce and reheat. Add more sugar or soy sauce to taste. Serve with rice. *Serves 8.*

BAKED HAM WITH MADEIRA

1 (10 to 12 lbs.) ham
1 cup brown sugar

1 teaspoon powdered cloves
2 cups Madeira

Simmer the ham for about 2½ hours. Cool. Preheat the oven to 350°. Remove the rind and excess fat from the ham. Rub in the sugar and powdered cloves. Put into a baking pan with 1 cup of the wine poured over, and bake for 40 minutes, basting several times. Add the remaining wine and raise the heat to 400°. Bake for half an hour more, basting frequently, until browned. *Serves 12 to 16.*

HAM SLICES IN RED WINE

2½ lbs. ham steaks, sliced ½-inch thick	2 tablespoons rendered ham or bacon fat, or butter
1 teaspoon sugar	
2 tablespoons prepared mustard	1 cup red wine

Rub the ham with sugar and mustard. Brown on both sides in the hot fat or butter in a heavy skillet, for about 10 minutes. Pour in the wine and cook, covered, for 5 minutes more. Transfer ham to a hot platter. Heat and stir the wine and juices and pour them over the ham. *Serves 6.*

BEEF KIDNEYS WITH WHITE WINE

2 to 3 pounds beef kidneys	1 cup dry white wine
2 tablespoons butter	½ cup heavy cream (optional)
1 onion, sliced thin	
½ teaspoon salt	1 to 2 tablespoons flour (optional)
¼ teaspoon pepper	
1 cup beef broth or consommé	

Soak the kidneys in salted water for several hours. Slice into pieces ½-inch thick, removing the hard center core and any fat. Sauté in butter with the onion for 2 minutes. Add the salt, pepper, broth, and wine. Cover and simmer for 15 minutes or cook, covered, in a 400° oven for about 40 minutes, until the kidneys are tender. Heat the cream and add to the kidneys; or thicken the juices with a little flour blended with ¼ cup water or broth. This is good served with rice, noodles, or on toast. *Serves 4 to 6.*

BEEF KIDNEYS WITH RED WINE

Proceed as for *Beef Kidneys with White Wine* substituting red wine for the white.

VEAL KIDNEYS

6 to 8 veal kidneys	¼ teaspoon pepper
1 large onion, chopped fine	1 cup broth or bouillon
¼ cup butter	1 cup red wine
2 tablespoons flour	½ teaspoon sugar
1 teaspoon salt	

Cut up the kidneys; remove the fat and hard center cores. Sauté the onion in the butter until it is light brown. Add the kidneys and cook 3 to 4 minutes. Sprinkle with flour, salt, and pepper. Add the broth slowly while stirring. Add the wine and sugar and simmer for 4 to 5 minutes, no more. *Serves 6*

LAMB KIDNEYS

Proceed as for *Veal Kidneys* substituting 12 lamb kidneys for the veal kidneys. Cut the kidneys in halves or quarters and remove the hard center cores before sautéing them.

LAMB OR VEAL KIDNEYS WITH MUSTARD SAUCE

12 to 16 lamb kidneys or
   6 to 8 veal kidneys
1½ teaspoons salt
½ teaspoon pepper
3 tablespoons butter
1 tablespoon imported prepared mustard

1 tablespoon flour
½ teaspoon sugar
3 tablespoons water
½ cup white wine
½ to 1 cup sour cream
Rice or toast

Slice the kidneys, removing the hard center cores. Sprinkle them with the salt and pepper and sauté them in butter over quite high heat for 3 minutes. Add the mustard, flour, and sugar. Stir thoroughly. Gradually stir in the water and then the wine. Bring to a boil. Taste for seasoning. You may want to add a little more mustard. Stir in the sour cream just before serving. Serve with rice or on toast. *Serves 6 to 8.*

PORK KIDNEYS IN WINE

6 pork kidneys
Salted water
2 tablespoons butter
4 slices cut-up bacon or
    ¼ pound salt pork,
    diced
½ cup red or white wine

½ teaspoon thyme
½ clove garlic, crushed
½ teaspoon salt
¼ teaspoon pepper
1 teaspoon prepared
    mustard

Skin the kidneys, slice, and remove the tough center cores. Put the slices into a saucepan with salted water to cover. Boil for 1 minute, drain, and repeat. Drain and sauté the kidneys in the butter with bacon or pork for 1 to 2 minutes. Add the wine, thyme, garlic, salt, and pepper and simmer, covered, for 15 to 20 minutes, until tender. Add the mustard and thicken the juices slightly, if you wish, with a flour-and-water paste. This is good with rice. *Serves 6.*

eggs

Eggs in wine are special.

EGGS HUNTER'S STYLE

½ pound chicken livers
4 tablespoons olive oil
¼ cup chopped onion
1¼ teaspoons salt
¼ teaspoon freshly ground
    black pepper
¼ teaspoon basil or thyme

½ cup peeled, chopped
    tomatoes
½ cup dry white wine
8 eggs
8 slices buttered toast
1 tablespoon parsley

Cut the livers in half. Heat the oil in a large skillet; sauté the chopped onion 3 minutes. Add the livers; sauté 5 minutes, stirring occasionally. Stir in the salt, pepper, herbs, tomatoes, and wine. Simmer for 5 minutes. Break the eggs into the pan, cover, and cook until set, about 3 minutes. Transfer each egg to a piece of toast and cover with the livers and sauce. Sprinkle with parsley. *Serves 4 to 8.*

EGGS AMANDINE

¼ cup butter
2 tablespoons minced onion
½ cup ground almonds
¼ cup boiled ham, ground
½ cup dry white wine

6 eggs
½ cup heavy cream
1 teaspoon salt
¼ teaspoon pepper
Patty shells or toast

Melt the butter in a skillet. Add the onion, almonds, and ham. Sauté for 5 minutes, stirring almost constantly. Add the wine, and simmer for 3 minutes while you beat together the eggs, cream, salt, and pepper in a bowl. Pour this over the almond mixture and cook to the desired consistency, stirring constantly. Do not overcook. Serve in patty shells or on toast squares. *Serves 4 to 6.*

SHIRRED EGGS WITH SHERRIED CHICKEN LIVERS

½ pound chicken livers
¼ cup butter
1 teaspoon salt
¼ teaspoon pepper
2 tablespoons minced onion

2 tablespoons flour
1 cup beef broth or bouillon
½ cup cream sherry or
    Madeira
12 eggs

Cut the livers into 2 or 3 pieces each and brown in 2 tablespoons of the butter. Sprinkle with ¼ teaspoon salt and ⅛ teaspoon pepper. When cooked, remove from pan and keep warm. Add the remaining butter to the pan and brown the onion for 1 minute. Stir in the flour and cook and stir until smooth. Gradually stir in the broth and then the wine. Grease 6 individual baking dishes and break 2 eggs into each. Cook under the broiler until whites are set. Meanwhile, return the livers to the wine sauce and reheat. Remove the eggs from the broiler and spoon some sauce and livers over. *Serves 6.*

vegetables

Wine makes roughage smooth whether in the form of *vegetables* or *salads*.

BROCCOLI WITH WHITE WINE

1 bunch broccoli	1 teaspoon salt
2 tablespoons olive oil	¼ teaspoon pepper
1 cup dry white wine	2 tablespoons melted butter
1 clove garlic, crushed	or olive oil

Cut off and discard about a half-inch of the stem ends of the broccoli. Scrape the tough stems with a vegetable scraper. Put broccoli into a pot with oil, wine, garlic, salt, and pepper. Cover. Cook until tender, about 15 minutes. Then arrange broccoli in a warm serving bowl and keep warm. Boil the liquid to reduce it to about half. Add the butter or oil and pour over the broccoli. *Serves 4.*

GREEK EGGPLANT

1 medium eggplant
2 teaspoons salt
½ cup olive oil
¾ cup dry white wine
1 bay leaf

¼ teaspoon thyme
¼ teaspoon pepper
1½ cups peeled, chopped
    tomatoes

Peel the eggplant, and cut as for French-fried potatoes. Sprinkle it with the salt, and let stand 30 minutes. Drain well. Heat the oil in a skillet and brown the eggplant. Remove it and set aside. To the oil remaining in the skillet, add the wine, bay leaf, thyme, pepper, and tomatoes. Simmer for 15 minutes. Return the eggplant to the skillet and cook over low heat for another 15 minutes. Serve cold. *Serves 4.*

SAUTÉED BEAN SPROUTS

2 tablespoons butter
2 scallions, minced
1 pound fresh bean sprouts,
    washed

2 tablespoons sugar
2 tablespoons soy sauce
1 tablespoon sherry
Rice

Sauté the scallions in the butter till not quite brown. Add the bean sprouts and toss over medium heat until tender but still crisp, about 10 minutes. Add sugar, soy sauce, and sherry, and simmer 2 or 3 minutes more. Add more sugar, soy sauce, and sherry to taste. Canned bean sprouts, washed and drained, may be substituted. Cooked pork or chicken, shredded, may be added to make an inexpensive main dish, served with rice. *Serves 4.*

RED CABBAGE WITH RED WINE

1 large firm red cabbage, shredded	½ cup red wine
	2 tablespoons sugar
1 cup minced onion	1 teaspoon salt
2 tablespoons butter	2 teaspoons cornstarch

Sauté the onion in butter until transparent but not browned. Add the cabbage, wine, sugar, and salt. Simmer, covered, for half an hour. Drain and reserve liquid. Place the cabbage in a serving dish and keep warm. Boil the liquid until it is reduced to about half a cup. Dissolve the cornstarch in a little cold water; stir it into the liquid, and cook until clear and thickened. Pour over the cabbage. *Serves 6.*

WEINKRAUT

3 tablespoons butter	2 apples, peeled and diced
1 medium onion, chopped	1 cup broth
1 quart sauerkraut, drained and washed	1 cup red or dry white wine
	2 teaspoons sugar

Combine all of the ingredients and simmer for an hour. Taste for seasoning. *Serves 4 to 6.*

POTATOES IN WHITE WINE

3 tablespoons butter	1 teaspoon salt
6 onions, chopped	¼ teaspoon pepper
8 to 10 medium potatoes, peeled and cut up	About 1 cup white wine

Melt the butter and sauté the onions until transparent. Add the potatoes, season with salt and pepper, and add wine to cover the potatoes. Cover and simmer for half an hour. Most of the wine will be absorbed. Reseason to taste. *Serves 6 to 8.*

MASHED SWEET POTATOES

Grated rind of 1 orange
2 tablespoons butter
¼ cup sherry

½ teaspoon salt
2 cups mashed sweet
  potatoes or yams

Add the other ingredients to the mashed sweet potatoes and season to taste. Beat until fluffy, pile them into a casserole and bake at 350° until they are lightly browned. *Serves 4.*

sauces and
salad dressings

Sauces and *salad dressings* are at their very best when made with wine.

WINE CREAM SAUCE

3 tablespoons butter
3 tablespoons flour
1 cup milk and 1 cup broth
  or 2 cups milk

¼ cup dry white or red wine
Salt
Pepper

Melt the butter and stir in the flour. Heat and stir until smooth. Gradually blend in the milk and broth. (If you use white wine, use a chicken or fish broth; if red, use beef broth.) Cook and stir until smooth, add the wine, and reheat. Add salt and pepper to taste. You will need less seasoning if using broth—more if you use only milk. *Yield: about 2 cups.*

SHERRY CREAM SAUCE

Substitute ¼ cup of dry sherry for the wine in *Wine Cream Sauce.*

BUTTER-WINE SAUCE

6 tablespoons butter
¼ cup flour
1 cup boiling water

¾ cup white wine
½ teaspoon salt
⅛ teaspoon pepper

Melt 4 tablespoons butter, blend in the flour, and when smooth, stir in the water gradually. When thickened and smooth, add the wine, salt, and pepper, and simmer 2 minutes. Just before serving add the remaining butter, cut into small pieces. Good with fish or vegetables. *Yield: about 2 cups.*

WHITE WINE SAUCE

3 tablespoons butter
¼ cup flour
1 cup chicken broth

1½ cups white wine
½ teaspoon salt

Melt the butter and blend in the flour. Stir in the broth gradually. When the sauce is thickened and smooth, add the wine and simmer for 2 or 3 minutes more. Add salt to taste. Good with poultry and vegetables. This is a thinner sauce than *Butter-Wine Sauce*. *Yield: about 2½ cups.*

SAUTERNE-BUTTER SAUCE

¼ cup butter
2 tablespoons minced
    shallots, onion, or
    scallions

1 teaspoon prepared
    mustard
1 tablespoon lemon juice
½ cup sauterne
½ teaspoon salt

Melt the butter and add the shallots, onion, or scallions. Cook for 1 minute and add the remaining ingredients. Simmer 2 minutes. Stir in the remaining butter and serve at once. Especially good for shellfish or fish. *Yield: about 1 cup.*

CURRANT JELLY SAUCE WITH
   MADEIRA

½ cup orange juice
Grated rind of 1 orange

1 cup currant jelly
⅓ cup Madeira

Heat the juice and rind, and stir in the jelly. When the sauce is smooth, add the wine. Serve hot with meats, poultry, or game. *Yield: about 2 cups.*

WINE HOLLANDAISE SAUCE

½ cup butter
1 teaspoon flour
4 egg yolks

1 to 2 tablespoons lemon
  juice
⅓ cup dry white wine

Heat the butter in a double boiler. Stir in the flour and add the egg yolks one at a time, stirring steadily. Stir in the lemon juice and wine. Keep stirring with a fork or small wire whisk for several minutes until thickened. Serve at once. Excellent for fish and vegetables. *Yield: about 1 cup.*

MAYONNAISE

1 egg yolk
½ teaspoon salt
½ teaspoon dry mustard

1 cup oil (including ⅓ cup
  olive oil)
2 tablespoons wine vinegar

Mix the egg yolk, salt, and mustard in a small bowl. Add the oil drop by drop while stirring constantly with a fork, whisk, or rotary beater. When the mixture begins to thicken, add the oil in a thin stream, continuing to stir. When the mayonnaise gets quite thick, add a little vinegar and then continue with the remaining oil and vinegar. Be sure to add the oil very slowly to start with, until it goes into solution with the egg. *Yield: about 1½ cups.*

BLENDER MAYONNAISE

1 egg
½ teaspoon salt
½ teaspoon dry mustard

1½ tablespoons wine
vinegar
¾ cup oil

Put the egg, salt, mustard, and vinegar in the blender. With the blender on at its lowest speed, add 2 tablespoons of the oil. Pour in the remaining oil in a slow stream while blending at low speed. This is foolproof and takes about 3 minutes. *Yield: about 1½ cups.*

WINE MAYONNAISE

3 tablespoons white wine
1 teaspoon lemon juice

1 cup *Mayonnaise*

Stir the wine and lemon juice into the *Mayonnaise*. *Yield: about 1¼ cups.*

HOT WINE MAYONNAISE

1 cup *Mayonnaise*
¼ cup sauterne
1 tablespoon lemon juice

2 tablespoons minced
parsley

Combine the ingredients and heat in a double boiler. Good on hot vegetables, potato salad, or beef. *Yield: about 1½ cups.*

CHAUD-FROID WINE SAUCE

1 envelope unflavored
    gelatin
3 tablespoons dry sherry or
    white wine

½ cup chicken broth
2 egg yolks

Soften the gelatin in the wine, add the broth, and heat and stir until the gelatin is dissolved. Beat the egg yolks in a double boiler. While stirring, pour in the wine-broth slowly. Cook about 3 minutes, until slightly thickened. Cool, stirring occasionally, until thick. Coat the meat to be covered with the sauce and chill. If coating fish, use canned shrimp or lobster bisque or fish broth or bottled clam juice instead of chicken broth. *Yield: about 1 cup.*

WHITE-WINE FRENCH DRESSING

½ teaspoon salt
⅛ teaspoon white pepper
1 teaspoon sugar
¼ teaspoon dry mustard
½ cup white wine

½ teaspoon grated onion
½ cup white wine vinegar
½ cup oil (at least half
    olive oil)

Mix the dry ingredients. Stir in the wine and then add the onion, vinegar, and oil. Mix thoroughly. *Yield: about 1¼ cups.*

RED-WINE FRENCH DRESSING

1 teaspoon salt
1 teaspoon sugar
½ teaspoon pepper
1 clove garlic cut in half

½ cup red wine
¼ cup red wine vinegar
1 cup oil (including some
   olive oil)

Mix the dry ingredients. Add the garlic. Pour in the wine and vinegar. Stir well and then add the oil. Shake in a jar with an ice cube in it. Remove garlic. *Yield: about 1¾ cups.*

SHERRY FRENCH DRESSING

½ teaspoon salt
1 teaspoon sugar
1 egg
¼ cup vinegar

1½ cups oil (at least ½
   cup olive oil)
½ cup sherry

Mix the salt, sugar, and egg. Add the vinegar, and then the oil slowly, while beating. Add the sherry in a slow stream while continuing to stir. *Yield: about 2½ cups.*

WHITE-WINE DESSERT SAUCE

¼ pound butter
¼ cup brown sugar

1 egg
½ cup white wine

Cream the butter and sugar together. Add the egg and beat until fluffy. Stir in the wine gradually. Cook and stir in a double boiler until thickened. *Yield: about 1 cup.*

RED-WINE DESSERT SAUCE

Proceed as for *White-Wine Dessert Sauce,* substituting red wine for white.

HARD SAUCE

¼ cup butter
1 cup superfine sugar

1 to 1½ tablespoons sweet
    sherry or port

Cream the butter until soft and light. Blend in the sugar a tablespoon at a time. Add the wine. Chill before serving. This is good with plum pudding and other puddings. *Yield: about 1 cup.*

desserts

"Make the end most sweet" with wine desserts.

ZABAGLIONE

8 egg yolks
½ cup powdered sugar

1¼ cups Marsala
Dash of cinnamon

Put the unbroken egg yolks in a chafing dish or double boiler. Cover them with powdered sugar and Marsala. Do not stir. The cover of sugar and wine keeps the eggs from drying. This much may be done ahead and then the zabaglione cooked at the table. To cook, stir the ingredients and put over boiling water. Stir and cook until thickened and foamy, 3 to 5 minutes. Serve warm in sherbet glasses, topped with cinnamon. *Serves 6.*

ZABAGLIONE PIE

Crust

1¼ cups graham-cracker crumbs (16 squares crushed)

¼ cup confectioners' sugar
1 teaspoon cinnamon
6 tablespoons melted butter

Filling

1 tablespoon unflavored gelatin
½ cup cold water
4 eggs

1 cup sugar
⅔ cup Marsala
½ teaspoon cinnamon
⅓ teaspoon salt

Preheat oven to 375°. Mix the crumbs, confectioners' sugar, and cinnamon with the melted butter. Pat into a thin layer in an 8-inch pie pan. Bake 15 minutes. Chill.

Soak the gelatin in the cold water. Separate the eggs. Put the yolks with half the sugar in the top of a double boiler and beat until light. Stir in the Marsala and cook over boiling water, stirring constantly, until the custard thickens. Add the cinnamon. Remove from heat, stir in the softened gelatin, and chill until it begins to set. Whip the egg whites until stiff, gradually adding the rest of the sugar and the salt. Whip the chilled custard and fold in the egg whites. Pile in the pie shell and sprinkle with cinnamon. Chill until set. Serve without delay, with or without sweetened whipped cream flavored with vanilla and topped with more cinnamon. *Serves 4 to 6.*

SHERRY CHIFFON PIE

Follow the recipe for *Zabaglione Pie,* substituting sherry for the Marsala.

FROZEN ZABAGLIONE

6 egg yolks
½ cup sugar
1 tablespoon grated lemon
    rind

1 cup Marsala or sweet
    sherry
½ envelope gelatin
½ pint heavy cream,
    whipped

Beat the egg yolks and sugar and add the lemon rind. Put into a double boiler with the wine. Soften the gelatin in a little water and add it to the eggs and wine. Cook and stir until thickened. Cool. Fold in the whipped cream and freeze in a serving dish or mold. *Serves 6 to 8.*

WHITE WINE CUSTARD

2 cups sweet white wine   ¾ cup sugar
    such as a sauterne or   6 egg yolks
    Barsac

Heat the wine and sugar until the sugar is dissolved. Remove from heat. Beat the egg yolks until thick and foamy. Pour slowly into the wine, stirring constantly. Pour into 6 custard cups. Put the cups in a pan of hot water (with water coming halfway up the cups). Bake at 350° for about 40 minutes, until a silver knife comes out clean. *Serves 6.*

CHOCOLATE MOUSSE

6 ounces semisweet or   1 tablespoon Instant or
    sweet chocolate   freeze-dried coffee
5 eggs, separated   Pinch salt
2 tablespoons red wine

Beat the egg yolks. Melt the chocolate in a double boiler. Cool it slightly and pour onto the beaten egg yolks. Stir. Be careful not to have the chocolate so hot that it scrambles the eggs. Stir in wine and instant coffee. Beat the egg whites and salt until stiff, and fold into the chocolate mixture. Pour into pot-de-crème cups, small custard cups, or a glass or chinaware serving bowl. Chill several hours. It is appropriate to use after-dinner coffee spoons or other small spoons with this rich dessert. *Serves 6 to 8.*

STRAWBERRIES WALDORF I

8 ounces cream cheese
¼ cup cream
2 tablespoons sugar

1 tablespoon rum or brandy
2 boxes strawberries

Smooth together the cheese, cream, sugar, and rum or brandy. Wash but do not hull the berries. Place a spoonful of the cheese mixture in the center of six dessert plates and surround it with the berries, hulls out. Chill. Each person dips his berries in the cheese mixture with his fingers. *Serves 6.*

STRAWBERRIES WALDORF II

Substitute 3 tablespoons brown sugar for the white, and add 1 tablespoon of a sweet white wine and omit the liquor in *Strawberries Waldorf I.*

RUBY STRAWBERRIES

2 packages frozen rasp-
    berries
¼ cup sugar
3 tablespoons red wine

1 tablespoon brandy
3 pints strawberries
½ cup toasted slivered
    almonds (garnish)

Thaw the raspberries slightly and buzz in a blender with 2 tablespoons of the sugar. Strain to remove seeds. Add wine and brandy. Wash and hull the strawberries. Sprinkle with the remaining sugar. Put the strawberries in a serving bowl, preferably a glass one, pour the raspberry sauce over, and chill until ready to serve. Garnish with almonds if you wish. *Serves 6.*

SHERRY JELLY

1 envelope gelatin
¼ cup cold water
1 cup hot water

¼ cup sugar
¾ cup sherry
Whipped cream (optional)

Soften the gelatin in the cold water. Add the hot water and sugar, and heat and stir until both are dissolved. Add the sherry and pour into a mold, a low bowl, or 4 individual dishes. Chill. Unmold or serve from the dishes. Serve topped with whipped cream, if you wish. *Serves 4.*

RED WINE JELLY

Substitute red wine for the sherry; add 1 tablespoon of lemon juice or ¼ cup of orange juice, and a little more sugar to taste in *Sherry Jelly.*

PLUMS IN WINE JELLY

1 (1 lb. 13 oz.) can purple,
     red, or greengage
     plums
2 envelopes gelatin

½ cup water
¾ to 1 cup red or rosé
     wine (white wine for
     greengage plums)

Drain the plums and measure the syrup; you need 1 to 1½ cups. Put the measured syrup in a pot. Pit the plums. Dissolve the gelatin in ½ cup of water and add the syrup. Add wine, heat and stir until gelatin is dissolved. Pour the syrup mixture over the plums. Pour into a mold or bowl and chill until firm. *Serves 4.*

MACÉDOINE OF FRESH FRUITS

1 quart strawberries
1 small pineapple
3 large oranges, sectioned

4 to 5 peaches (if available)
Superfine sugar
½ cup Madeira

Wash, hull, and sugar the berries. Peel the pineapple and cut into bite-size pieces. Peel and section the oranges, being sure to remove all the membrane. Peel, pit, and slice the peaches. Mix all of the fruit together and add sugar to taste. Pour the Madeira over the fruit and toss very gently. *Serves 8 to 10.*

CANNED FRUITS WITH SHERRY SAUCE

1 (16 oz.) can pears
1 (16 oz.) can peaches
1 (16 oz.) can Bing cherries
1 (16 oz.) can pineapple
   pieces

2 cups mixed syrup from
   the above fruits
¾ cup sugar
¼ cup sweet sherry or
   Madeira

Combine any 3 cans of fruit. Drain and blend liquids. To make the sauce, simmer 2 cups of the liquid with sugar until thickened, about 10 minutes. Cool and add the sherry or Madeira. Pour over fruits and chill in refrigerator for several hours. *Serves 6 to 8.*

PRUNES WITH WINE

1 pound dried prunes
1½ cups sugar

¼ cup strong red wine

Soak the prunes in water just to cover for several hours. Drain, reserving the water. There should be about 2 cups. Add the sugar to the water and boil 5 minutes. Add the prunes and simmer until soft and the juice is thickened. Add the wine. Chill. *Serves 6.*

APRICOTS WITH WHITE WINE

16 very ripe apricots
3 tablespoons red or white
   wine

3 ounces Curaçao or
   Cointreau

Plunge the apricots into boiling water for a moment. Cool under running water and slip the skins off. Slice them or cut thin into a bowl. Pour the wine and liqueur over. Chill. This dessert may be made with drained canned apricot halves. *Serves 6.*

CANTALOUPE WITH HONEY AND PORT

3 medium cantaloupes
3 tablespoons honey

1 to 1½ cups port wine

Cut the melons in half and remove the seeds. Combine the honey and wine and fill the center of each half. Chill. *Serves 6.*

part three

the partners:
wine
and
cheese

This book is not concerned with one-upmanship. It does not aim to make you an instant wine connoisseur, or even to teach you how to talk a good game. Wine is good to cook with, wine is good to drink, and that's what to do about wine, not talk about it. You don't want to be like that famous chump in the cartoon who simpered:

"It's just a simple little domestic wine, but I think you'll be amused at its effrontery."

You can safely ignore the effrontery of the "experts." Wine is not a religion, and there are no taboos involved. Drink what you like, with what you like, as you like it—and don't be intimidated by the wiseacres and the rules they lay down. You are not obliged to follow them.

If there are no rules you can't break when you feel like it, there are, however, certain areas of general agreement. You'll probably find, as most people do, that white wine and rosé wine are best chilled; red wine is best at room temperature. You'll probably like a white table wine with fish or chicken. Rhine wine,

Moselle, or Riesling is particularly appropriate to fish. A heavier white, such as Chablis or Montrachet, goes with chicken or other white meats such as veal, as well as fish. A red Burgundy or Bordeaux augments the taste of red meat and game. Pasta loves Italian chianti. Rosé goes with everything. Sweet wines accompany dessert and fruit. There you have a wide choice: sauterne, Muscatel, Barsac, port, Madeira, and Marsala. Red wine with cheese pleases most people.

Sparkling wines are for sparkling occasions: sparkling rosé, sparkling Burgundy, and sparkling Catawba. The queen of sparklers is champagne. If it's a champagne occasion, you may serve the sparkling vintage with dessert or throughout the meal, or even begin with it as an apéritif.

Americans are learning the gracious art of taking an apéritif before a meal in the European manner, instead of hard liquor. A glass of the wine to be served at dinner gently prepares the appetite for libations to follow. Some people like a sherry, au naturel or on the rocks. Still others prefer a vermouth, French or Italian, perhaps with a dash of bitters. Italian apéritifs, such as Campari and Punt e Mes, are bitter enough by themselves.

Choosing Wine

What kind of wine is best to buy? There is no set rule. Buy what you like and what you can afford. You don't have to serve French vintage wines that cost the eyes out of your head, as the French themselves put it, though it's fun to enjoy them now and then, on special occasions. For everyday, there are less costly and entirely agreeable wines to be had.

Touring the provinces of France, you would make a point of drinking the wine of the countryside, the *vin du pays*. Why not do it here? The wine of this country

—from Ohio, New York, or California—is equally a unique product, and equally an enjoyable one, without being too much over-priced. The same is true of table wines from Spain, Portugal, Italy, France, Germany, and Greece—not to mention Chile.

A good wine merchant will help you choose among vintages. He knows his merchandise. Tell him what you want to spend. If he wants your business, he will recommend the best he has in that price range. The probability is that he knows wines better than all your amateur advisors put together, so listen to him and learn. If he suggests selling you your wine by the case, you will be wise to follow his advice, because wine is cheaper by the dozen.

Storing Wine

When you have chosen your wine and thriftily bought it by the case, the question of storage arises. Where are you going to put it?

If you answer, "In the wine cellar!"—lucky you! You can skip this section.

But there aren't many real wine cellars around these days. The suburban split-level has a cubbyhole full of gadgets and a rumpus room, but no wine cellar. Nor has the city dweller such an appurtenance in his basement. The janitor won't let him.

Fortunately, a wine cellar needn't be in the cellar. True, the ideal temperature for wine is about 60°, which Americans don't think is the ideal temperature for people. However, a somewhat higher level of warmth does no harm in the short run, if the temperature holds reasonably constant. So don't hesitate to house your wine in a kitchen cabinet or on the upper shelf of a storage closet.

Only horses rest standing up. Wine likes to lie on its side, so the cork can keep moist. For that you need a wine rack. You can purchase one for little money. However, the case the wine comes in will cost you even less; namely nothing. Remove the cover, and lay the case on its side, and *voila!* You have a rack for twelve wine bottles, each separately nested and ready to be pulled out without disturbing its neighbor.

Serving Wine

Serving wine has its amenities, on which you will spend some time and thought.

Select a wine according to the menu you plan. Choose the right bottle long enough ahead to give it the proper treatment. White wine should go into the refrigerator to chill the first thing in the morning. Red wines are drunk at room temperature, which is no problem. A vintage red wine is customarily uncorked about an hour before serving, so that it can "breathe."

It is a ritual, a nice touch, for the host to pour an inch of the wine into his own glass first, and sample it. Now that the Borgias are no longer giving dinner parties, this ceremony is not necessary to assure the guests that the wine has not been spiked with a lethal dose of Aqua Tofana; but if the wine has turned, this is the moment to find it out. It saves washing a round of wine glasses.

Approving the vintage, the host now pours some wine into each glass. If he gives the bottle a slight turn as he stops pouring, he will prevent the dripping drop that stains the tablecloth.

The right wine glass seems to enhance the wine. I don't say you have to throw away the colorful goblets you have, the wedding presents, the souvenirs of Mexico, Venice, and Czechoslovakia. No doubt they are conversation pieces. But when you go to buy glasses for wine, remember that wine is a beautiful color, and speaks for itself best in clear crystal.

The usual serving of wine is about three ounces; but don't go looking for three-ounce glasses. Wine likes space for its bouquet to gather. Choose larger glasses and fill them half full, rather on the principle of the brandy snifter.

To complete the ritual, the guests will savor the fragrance, sample the wine, and drink a toast to the host.

Eating Cheese

Wine enhances every kind of food. Wine and cheese are natural partners. Eating cheese is good, and best of all when the flavor is brought out by drinking wine with it. Not even "bread and cheese and kisses" can compete with bread and cheese and wine.

This menu plays no favorites, for cheese is enjoyed equally by old and young, rich and poor, farmer and city dweller, gourmet and glutton, man, woman, and mouse.

Eating cheese is a boon to the homemaker and her family, the hostess and her guests, for ease, nourishment, economy, pleasure, and distinction. Choose it, serve it, and eat it; it's as simple as that!

Cheeses for eating come in bewildering variety; you can eat cheese every day for half a year and not repeat yourself once. And think of the fun you would have, and the money you would save!

When you come to make a choice among all those cheeses, you needn't let it bewilder you. The many, many varieties of eating-cheeses fall into only five categories. In general, when assembling cheeses for eating, it is well to combine categories—firm with soft or mild with pungent and spicy. Here is a partial list of the five kinds of cheeses:

MILD, SOFT: cottage cheese, cream cheese, Neufchâtel

PUNGENT, SOFT: Brie, Camembert, Liederkranz, Limburger

SEMI-SOFT: Port du Salut, Bel Paese, Muenster, Tilsit

FIRM: Edam, Gouda, Fontina, Monterey Jack, Feta, Cheddar (mild to sharp), Swiss, Emmenthaler, Gruyère

PUNGENT, BLUE-VEINED: Stilton, Roquefort, Gorgonzola, Blue

A sixth category, hard cheeses, is more for cooking than for eating—including as it does Parmesan and Romano.

These days, very satisfactory pungent, soft cheeses are imported in cans from Denmark, Germany and France. English Cheddar mixed with port wine is often brought over in crocks, and it makes distinguished eating.

Process cheese (cheese mixed with milk solids) and cheese spreads abound and please many. Cheeses and cheese spreads are put forth flavored with a great variety of things: caraway seeds, bacon bits, pimento, providing a change if you get tired of the straight taste of cheese. But that isn't likely to happen in a hurry.

A great advantage of cheese is its keeping qualities. It keeps very well in a cold place. A whole cheese keeps best. Once you have cut it, you must protect it from drying out. You can wrap it in plastic wrap or foil.

Cold cheese is cold comfort. Cheese must be served at room temperature. If it's in the refrigerator, take it out in the morning and let it stand a while to mellow. Firm cheese will cut better and taste more savory; soft cheeses like Brie and Camembert will deliquesce to just the right runny consistency and release all their pungency to nose and palate. That's cheese at its best.

Cheese-and-Wine Parties

PARTIES WITHOUT KITCHEN FACILITIES. When you want to give a party, and you have absolutely no facilities, cheese and wine are the answer. All you need is a hunk of cheese, a box of crackers, a knife, a bottle of wine and some glasses.

Suppose you want to stage an office party; you don't want to fuss around with dishes and cutlery to tote and wash up. Cheese is the choice! If it's a cozy celebration, not involving too many people, one large and noble piece of Swiss or Cheddar or Port du Salut will look impressive and fill both the bill and the customers. A box of crackers and a bottle of red wine agreeably round out the menu. The new plastic wine glasses are handsome to look at, pleasant to handle, and disposable. If you want to get formal, add paper plates and paper napkins, and you can partify with ease.

If it's a large party, now is the time for a cheese platter. A large round Brie beside the block of Port du Salut or Swiss, plus a crock of flavored Cheddar or a whole Stilton, will look generous and vanish rapidly. Don't crowd these goodies onto a small tray. Allow plenty of space for cutting and laying out slices as the party progresses.

These days there is almost as great a variety of crackers as cheeses. Offer several different kinds. And when you are opening more than one bottle of wine, why not offer a choice of red and white?

Variety is the keynote, and with so many cheeses, so many kinds of crackers, and so many wines available, the office party-maker needn't ever get repetitious.

The following menus suggest a few of the many, many cheese-and-wine combinations.

RED AND/OR WHITE BURGUNDY	Mild Cheddar, Blue cheese, Neufchâtel, Fontina; Ritz crackers, Melba toast, soda crackers

RED BORDEAUX AND/OR RHINE WINE	Swiss, Edam, Camembert, sharp Cheddar, Stilton; sesame-seed wafers, Melba rounds, Saltines
CHIANTI AND/OR SAUTERNE	Emmenthaler, Gorgonzola, Monterey Jack, Brie; rye flatbread, soda crackers, hard water crackers

EASY PARTIES AT HOME. Why shouldn't you take it easy at home as well as at the office? It's true you have more facilities at home, but why not avail yourself of the cheese-with-ease idea there as well? It's an ideal kind of party to come home to. After the game, after the theater, after the concert, you don't want to come home and fuss. If it's a cheese-and-wine party, you won't have to. Open the door, and there is your party waiting for you: a handsome cheese platter keeping fresh under plastic wrap, an opened red wine "breathing" or white wine chilling in the refrigerator, crackers already arranged on trays. Because you are at home, you can add a luxury or two, like breads of various kinds including pumpernickel and a crusty French. If you add fruit, how beautiful it looks as a centerpiece, and how good it tastes, fresh and faintly sweet, setting off the cheese.

These menus suggest what you can do to make an easy cheese-and-wine-party at home.

RED OR WHITE BORDEAUX	Brie, Port du Salut, cream cheese with currant jelly Bartlett pears Hard rolls, water crackers
RED BURGUNDY	Camembert, Neufchâtel, sharp Cheddar Apples French bread, pumpernickel

SAUTERNE OR ROSÉ   Bel Paese, Roquefort, Gruyère
Winter pears
Italian bread, toasted rolls

SPECIAL PARTIES: WINE-TASTINGS. For wine lovers and learners alike, nothing is more fun than a wine-tasting party. Here the whole point is the wine, but the cheese is necessary, too, to clear the palate and bring out the bouquet of the wines. You should choose a firm, mild cheese—an American Cheddar, a Swiss or Emmenthaler, a mild Canadian Cheddar like Mt. St. Bénoit, an Edam or Gouda. One is enough. Cube it into bite-size pieces for the fingers to lift.

Don't omit breadstuffs. Salted crackers are taboo. Water crackers or soda crackers will do. Crusty bread —French or Italian—cut into small cubes is good.

All this is on the side. The wine takes the spotlight. You may present about six wines for tasting. Any more will bring confusion. It is well to avoid too great a variety in the choices. The rule is to keep to wines all made from the same kind of grape, as suggested in the lists to come.

The order of business is simple. Each guest savors a sample of wine, and then with a bit of bread and cheese he clears his taste buds for the next sample. And so on, all evening; for a wine-tasting party is not only a gustatory pleasure, it's an evening's entertainment as well.

If after the evening is over and all the kinds have been thoroughly tried, you take a popularity poll, you may be surprised. It's unlikely the same wine will head every list.

Advanced wine drinkers might like to try themselves with a blindfold test. With large napkins you blindfold —not the drinkers, but the bottles—and then challenge the tasters to identify each wine. Only the most experienced palates can recognize every type, let alone every vineyard and every vintage. But it's fun, and educational, to try.

Here are suggested wine lists for your wine-tasting party.

RED BORDEAUX	Château Latour Château Lynch Bages Château Calon Ségur Sauvignon (Heitz Cellars) Cabernet (Brother Timothy) Zinfandel (Louis Martini)
RED BURGUNDY	Vosne-Romanée Côtes de Beaune-Villages Châteauneuf-du-Pape Pinot Noir (Sonoma) Petit Sirah (Napa) Pinot (Almaden)
WHITE RHINE WINE	Schloss Johannisberger Bernkasteler Riesling Niersteiner Traminer (Buena Vista) White Riesling (Z.D.) Sylvaner (Christian Brothers)
WHITE BURGUNDY	Pouilly Fuissé Chablis Montrachet Pinot Blanc (Gallo) Pinot Chardonnay (Beaulieux) Sémillion (Paul Masson)
BEAUJOLAIS	Beaujolais-Villages Moulin-à-Vent Fleurie Gamay (Napa) Beaujolais (Wente Brothers) Gamay Beaujolais (Paul Masson)

SPECIAL PARTIES: FONDUE PARTIES. Fondue *is* cheese and wine. Fondue is a French word meaning "melted," and that is exactly what a fondue is: cheese melted with wine and other things. A fondue party is the ultimate in do-it-yourself and eat-it-yourself, and that is why it is so popular these days. You do it yourself in your fondue pot at table, and you eat it yourself with your long fondue fork, spearing a bit of crusty French bread, stirring it in the hot cheese mixture, and bringing it out dripping—from pot to mouth in one simple twist of the wrist, and no stopovers on the way. What could be simpler?

Perhaps you haven't got one of those fashionable fondue sets. You don't need one. For cooking up the savory sauce and keeping it hot (which is a must), your chafing dish will do very well. Or you can use any casserole on the stove and then keep it warm at table over a hot plate or a candle-warmer.

He who eats with the devil, they say, must have a long fork. Since you don't plan on having such a guest, perhaps you don't have any long forks. For the fondue party, you can substitute Chinese bamboo sticks, or kebab sticks, or even ordinary dinner forks. Anything will do that gets the bits of bread into the pot deep enough to cover them with the delicious fondue.

Since fondue is made with wine, offer the same wine to drink with it.

SWISS FONDUE I

1 clove garlic, split	¼ teaspoon salt
2 cups dry white wine	⅛ teaspoon pepper
1 pound Swiss cheese, shredded or coarsely grated	⅛ teaspoon nutmeg
	½ cup kirsch
3 tablespoons flour	French bread or hard rolls

Rub a fondue pot or heavy casserole with the split garlic. Pour in the wine and heat it. Combine the cheese and flour and add them gradually to the wine while stirring. When all the cheese is in and is bubbling, add the seasonings and the kirsch. Keep the fondue simmering. Serve with pieces of bread and let each person "dunk" his own, using a long (fondue) fork. Don't miss the hard crust that forms at the bottom of the pot when the fondue is almost gone! *Serves 4.*

SWISS FONDUE II

1 clove garlic, split
2 cups white wine
1½ pounds shredded Swiss
    cheese (about 6 cups)

¼ cup flour
Chunks of French bread

Rub the fondue pot with the split garlic. Heat the wine in the pot. Toss the cheese with the flour and stir it slowly into the wine, using a wooden spoon. When the cheese is melted and bubbling, each person spears pieces of crusty bread and dips them into the fondue. Keep the fondue very hot until it is all used up. *Serves 6.*

CHEDDAR FONDUE I

½ pound cheddar-type
    cheese, cut up
1 stick (½ cup) butter
6 eggs, beaten

Salt
Pepper
Worcestershire sauce
French bread or hard rolls

Melt the cheese while stirring and add the butter. Beat the eggs. Stir a little cheese into the eggs and return all to the fondue pot. Cook and stir until smooth. Add salt and pepper and Worcestershire sauce to taste. Serve bubbly hot with pieces of French bread or cut-up hard rolls. Have a long fork for each to dip his bread into the cheese. *Serves 4 to 6.*

CHEDDAR FONDUE II

1 cup red wine	½ cup milk
1 pound Cheddar cheese, cut up or shredded	½ teaspoon salt
	Pinch pepper
¼ cup butter	Chunks of French or Italian bread
6 eggs	

Heat the wine in an ovenproof dish or casserole. Stir in the cheese a little at a time. Add the butter. Mix the eggs with milk and stir in gradually. Season the fondue with salt and pepper. Keep it bubbling hot and serve with pieces of French or Italian bread and long forks. *Serves 6.*

TOMATO-CHEESE FONDUE

1 (1⅜ oz.) package onion soup mix	½ teaspoon Worcestershire sauce
2 cups tomato juice	French or rye bread, cut into cubes
1 teaspoon lemon juice	
1½ pounds Cheddar cheese, shredded	

Put the onion soup mix, and the tomato and lemon juices in a fondue pot. When simmering, add the cheese gradually while stirring. Add Worcestershire sauce and correct the seasoning. Spear cubes of French or crusty rye bread with long forks and dip them into the bubbling pot. *Serves 6.*

ITALIAN CHEESE FONDUE

1¾ pounds Fontina cheese,
    diced (substitute
    Gruyère if you have to)
Milk to cover
4 eggs, beaten
¼ cup butter

½ teaspoon salt
¼ teaspoon pepper
Thinly sliced white truffles
    (optional)
Toast

Put the cut-up cheese in milk and let stand several hours. Put the eggs in a double boiler or fondue dish with the cheese and any milk which has not been absorbed. Add butter, salt, and pepper. Cook, stirring constantly, until thick and smooth. Add the truffles for an unusual treat. Serve at once in a heated dish with toast cut into bite-size pieces. *Serves 6.*

SAUTERNE FONDUE

1 pound Swiss cheese,
    diced or shredded
½ pound Gruyère cheese,
    diced or shredded
1 tablespoon cornstarch
1 clove garlic, split

1 cup sauterne
1 teaspoon lemon juice
1 tablespoon brandy
Dash pepper
Steamed new potatoes or
    cubes of French bread

Combine the cheeses and cornstarch. Rub the fondue pot with the split garlic. Pour the wine and lemon juice into the pot. When they are simmering, add the cheese, a scant cup at a time. After each addition, stir until melted. Add brandy and pepper and keep the pot simmering gently. Dip steamed potatoes or bread cubes into fondue with long forks. *Serves 6.*

CHAMPAGNE FONDUE

1 pound Swiss cheese,
  diced
2 tablespoons cornstarch
2 cups champagne

1 teaspoon lemon juice
Pinch salt
Pinch white pepper
French bread, cut into cubes

Mix the cheese and cornstarch. Pour the champagne into a fondue pot. Heat but do not boil. Add the cheese a little at a time, while stirring. Cook and stir until all is melted and smooth. Stir in the lemon juice, salt, and pepper. Serve with cubes of French bread and supply long forks. *Serves 4.*

MILK FONDUE

2 tablespoons butter
¼ cup flour
4 cups milk
1 pound Swiss cheese,
  grated

Pinch nutmeg
French bread in bite-size
  pieces

Melt the butter in a fondue pot, add the flour, and stir until blended. Pour in the milk slowly while stirring. Add the cheese a cup at a time, stirring steadily. Season with nutmeg. When smooth, serve with pieces of French bread and fondue forks. *Serves 4 to 6.*

RACLETTE

1½ to 2 pounds Raclette cheese	Dill pickles (optional)
2 pounds hot boiled new potatoes, skins on	

If you have a way to melt cheese at the table in a special Raclette stove, do so. (That's the way it's done in Switzerland.) If not, cut the cheese in slices, put them in a shallow pan or baking dish, and bake until the cheese melts, about 5 minutes. Leave the cheese in the hot dish. Let each person peel his own potatoes and cover them with melted cheese. If the cheese gets cool, put it in the oven for a few minutes. Raclette is often served with dill pickles. *Serves 4 to 6.*

FONDUE BOURGUIGNON

2 pounds lean, boneless, tender beef, sirloin, fillet or porterhouse, cut into ¾-inch cubes	3 tablespoons butter
	Red-Wine Sauce for Fondue
	Mustard-White Wine Sauce for Fondue
1 cup any vegetable oil	

Divide the raw beef among 4 to 6 plates. Heat the oil and butter until bubbly. This is best done in a chafing dish or fondue pot. Provide the sauces and long forks. Each person dips his beef into the bubbling pot for a few minutes, to the degree of doneness he wishes. 1 minute is rare; 2 minutes, medium. *Serves 4 to 6.*

RED WINE SAUCE FOR FONDUE

¾ cup red wine
½ cup beef broth or
    bouillon
2 tablespoons minced
    scallions

½ tablespoon minced
    parsley
¼ teaspoon sugar
¼ cup soft butter

Simmer the wine, broth, scallions, sugar, and parsley a few minutes, uncovered, until the liquid is reduced. Mix with the butter. *Yield: about 1 cup.*

MUSTARD-WHITE WINE SAUCE
FOR FONDUE

½ cup heavy or sour cream
3 tablespoons prepared
    mustard

½ teaspoon sugar
4 tablespoons dry white
    wine

Combine the ingredients. If too pungent, add a little more wine; if not pungent enough, add more mustard to taste. *Yield: about 1 cup.*

Swiss fondue has a near relative in the Welsh Rabbit, which is not a rabbit, but a savory cheese concoction. The name of the latter is an unkind joke on the poor silly Welsh—insinuating that they are too poor to eat meat, so they eat cheese and pretend it's meat. It was probably a Welshman who changed the name to a Welsh "rare bit," which it certainly is. The name of Irish Rabbit, another delicious cheese dish, is a similar joke on the Hibernians. English Monkey was undoubtedly named in retaliation.

WELSH RABBIT

¼ cup butter	2 teaspoons Worcestershire
½ cup flour	sauce
½ teaspoon salt	¾ pound Cheddar cheese,
¼ teaspoon dry mustard	shredded
2 cups milk	Toast

Melt the butter in a double boiler and blend in the flour, salt, and mustard. Stir in the milk slowly. Cook until thickened and smooth. Add the Worcestershire sauce and cheese. Continue to stir and cook until the cheese is melted. Serve on toast. *Serves 6.*

IRISH RABBIT

1 tablespoon chopped onion	1 teaspoon salt
1 tablespoon butter	1 egg
½ cup tomato sauce	2 tablespoons half-and-half
¾ pound mild Cheddar cheese, shredded	Toast

Simmer the onion gently in the butter for 2 or 3 minutes while stirring. Add the tomato sauce and cook 3 minutes. Add the cheese and salt and stir over low heat until the cheese is melted. Beat the egg into the half-and-half and add it to the cheese mixture. Reheat and serve on toast. *Serves 4 to 6.*

ENGLISH MONKEY

1 cup seasoned bread
    crumbs
1 cup milk
1 tablespoon butter
½ pound mild Cheddar
    cheese, shredded

1 egg, slightly beaten
Pinch cayenne
Toasted crackers or toast

Soak the bread crumbs in milk. Melt the butter and stir in the cheese. When the cheese has melted, add the bread crumbs (the milk will have been absorbed), the egg, and the cayenne. Cook 2 to 3 minutes. Serve on toasted crackers or toast. *Serves 4.*

TOMATO RABBIT

3 tablespoons butter
3 tablespoons flour
1 cup half-and-half
1 cup strained canned
    tomatoes
½ pound mild Cheddar
    cheese, shredded

2 eggs, slightly beaten
1 teaspoon salt
Pinch sugar
¼ teaspoon prepared
    mustard
⅛ teaspoon cayenne
Toast

Melt the butter, add the flour, and stir in the half-and-half slowly. Add the tomatoes and cheese. Stir until the cheese is melted. Stir in the eggs and season the rabbit with salt, sugar, mustard, and cayenne. Serve bubbling hot on toast. *Serves 4 to 6.*

BEER RABBIT

1 pound mild Cheddar
   cheese, shredded
1 cup beer
1 teaspoon dry mustard

1 teaspoon Worcestershire
   sauce
Toast

Melt the cheese over low heat in a double boiler or a chafing dish. Stir in the beer, mustard, and Worcestershire sauce. Cook and stir until the cheese is melted and the rabbit is smooth. Serve on toast. *Serves 4 to 6.*

STOUT RABBIT

1½ pounds sharp Cheddar,
   shredded
6 tablespoons butter
9 tablespoons flour
2 (11.39 oz.) bottles Guin-
   ness Stout

1½ teaspoons Worcester-
   shire sauce
Toast

To the shredded cheese in a saucepan add the butter, flour, Stout and Worcestershire sauce. Stir over medium heat until the rabbit bubbles gently and becomes smooth. Serve at once on buttered toast. *Serves 6.*

Wine with Your Meals

Drinking wine is an art. At its simplest, the picture is painted in two colors. It is easy to say, drink wine with your cheese at a cheese-platter party, or eat cheese with your wine at a wine-tasting affair. But choosing and combining your colors when you plan a whole meal becomes more complex as it becomes more interesting. From all the range of possible dishes, from all the variety of available wines, just which can be combined to best advantage into one harmonious whole? In the end, *you* are the artist, and the finished picture is *your* masterpiece.

The following menus can only suggest how you can bring together cheese and wine dishes and their complements with just the right wines for artistic eating and drinking. On any menu, American wines can always take the place of the French wines suggested.

WINE WITH THE BUFFET. Fork food goes on the buffet, "covered-dish" type casseroles which are so often made piquant with wine and cheese. A cheese platter is always appropriate too, and goes well with fruit or a fruity dessert. Salads may appear, and there is no law against cookies or cake!

BUFFET LUNCHEONS. Buffet luncheons feature light but savory dishes made with cheese or wine or both, and wines to suit.

MOSELLE

SUNRISE SALAD with LORENZO
DRESSING
Hot French bread
Cheese platter: Brie, Blue, Muen-
ster
APRICOTS WITH WHITE WINE

RED BURGUNDY

ASPARAGUS JUDGE TRUAX
Toasted English muffins
Cheese platter: sharp Cheddar,
Tilsit, Gorgonzola
RED WINE JELLY

CHABLIS

CHICKEN CASSEROLE WITH WHITE
WINE
GREEN BEANS AU GRATIN
Melba toast
Cheese platter: Port du Salut,
Emmenthaler, Crèma Danica
CANNED FRUITS WITH SHERRY
SAUCE

BUFFET DINNERS. Offer more choices, and more sub-
stantial viands, with a wider range of possible wines.
Cheese is sure to be one of the choices.

RED BURGUNDY

BEEF BOURGUIGNON
Noodles
CAULIFLOWER POLONAISE
GARLIC CHEESE BREAD I
Cheese platter: mild Cheddar,
Liederkranz, Roquefort
Pears and apples

WHITE BORDEAUX	JELLIED TOMATO-SHERRY SOUP
	CHICKEN TETRAZZINI
	BROCCOLI WITH WHITE WINE
	Toasted crackers
	Cheese platter: Emmenthaler, Port du Salut, cream cheese
	Grapes and cherries
RED BORDEAUX	EGGS IN ASPIC
	BEEF-AND-VEAL PATTIES IN WINE
	BAKED SPINACH AND CHEESE
	Sliced tomatoes with herbs
	Hard rolls
	Cheese platter: Gorgonzola, Bel Paese, Neufchâtel
	CHOCOLATE SOUFFLÉ
RHINE WINE	PATÉ IN ASPIC
	FISH FILLETS IN WINE
	Boiled new parsley potatoes
	Swedish cucumbers
	Toasted water crackers
	Cheese platter: mild American cheese, Brie, Stilton
	STRAWBERRIES WALDORF

LATE-NIGHT SUPPERS. Late-night suppers are for hungry people. One big tureen or salad bowl or casserole is called for, flanked by some kind of breadstuff, fruit, and/or something sweet. Add a cheese platter if you wish.

ROSÉ	BELGIAN CHICKEN
	CHEESE BISCUITS
	GREEN SALAD WITH SHERRY FRENCH DRESSING
	CHEESE TART

RHINE WINE	FISH SOUP
	GARLIC CHEESE BREAD II
	RUBY STRAWBERRIES
RED BORDEAUX	CHEF'S SALAD
	CHEESE STRAWS
	SHERRY CHIFFON PIE
RED CHIANTI	ELBOW MACARONI AND CHEESE CASSEROLE
	APPLE AND PEAR SALAD, PEACH OR NECTARINE SALAD
	SHERRY JELLY

WINE ON THE TABLE. The sit-down dinner is the largest canvas that the hostess paints, and the sit-down luncheon is not far behind. The choice of dishes that can be consumed at table is the widest, and when more than one wine is offered as the courses follow one another, some unusual combinations may result.

SIT-DOWN LUNCHEON MENUS

WHITE CHIANTI	CHILLED PEACH-WINE SOUP
	LINGUINE WITH WHITE CLAM SAUCE
	TOMATOES WITH MAYONNAISE
	WHITE WINE CUSTARD
ROSÉ	CHICKEN DIVAN
	Sliced herbed tomatoes
	Toasted English muffins
	MACÉDOINE OF FRESH FRUITS

WHITE BORDEAUX	TROUT IN WINE ASPIC Cucumbers in sour cream Popovers BAVARIAN CHEESE MOLD
WHITE BURGUNDY	SHRIMP SOUFFLÉ Green salad with ROQUEFORT-TOMATO DRESSING French bread CANTALOUPE WITH HONEY AND PORT

SIT-DOWN DINNER MENUS

HOCHHEIMER	TOMATO-CLAM SOUP
PINOT NOIR	BAKED HAM WITH MADEIRA MASHED SWEET POTATOES Cole slaw
SAUTERNE	COEUR À LA CRÈME with Strawberries

LIEBFRAUMILCH	MUSHROOM SOUP
MONTRACHET	TONGUE IN WHITE WINE Spinach
CHÂTEAU LATOUR	CHOCOLATE CHEESECAKE

DRY SHERRY	Consommé with sherry (hot or cold)

RED BORDEAUX	DUCK WITH ORANGE AND PORT WINE
	WEINKRAUT
	Dumplings
BARSAC	RHUBARB PIE

BEAUJOLAIS	BROILED GRAPEFRUIT
	KEBABS IN MARINADE
	Rice or wheat pilaf
	Green salad with ROQUEFORT-TOMATO DRESSING
RED BORDEAUX	CHEESECAKE

CHIANTI	FETTUCINE ALFREDO
CHABLIS	SHRIMPS DE JONGHE
	BRAISED ENDIVE
	GREEK EGGPLANT
	ZABAGLIONE

They sound good, don't they? And what with the special money-saving qualities of cheese and wine cookery, they are not too expensive.

Just once, how would you like to shoot the works and go out in a blaze of glory?

DINNER DELUXE

Champagne	Maine lobster mayonnaise
Romanée-Conti	Beef Wellington
	Fonds d'artichauts avec petits pois
	Hearts of palm with Bibb lettuce, vinaigrette
Chateau d'Yquem	Fraises des bois à la crème fraîche

After that, you might have to live on bread and cheese for the rest of the year; but that's good eating too!

A plate of cheeses underneath the bough,
A loaf of bread, a jug of wine, and thou
Beside me lunching in the wilderness—
Ah, wilderness were Paradise enow!

a glossary of cheeses

BEL PAESE
mild, soft to medium, creamy texture, light cream color

BLUE
tangy, distinctive piquant flavor, semi-soft and crumbly, white with blue veins

BRIE
semi-mild to pungent, soft and smooth, creamy yellow

BOURSIN
mild and flavorful, soft, creamy white

CAMEMBERT
mild to pungent, smooth and soft, creamy yellow

CHEDDAR (often called American)
Mild, medium, sharp, and very sharp, smooth and firm, yellow to orange

COTTAGE
mild, soft, small to large curds, white

CREAM
mild, soft, smooth, white

EDAM
nutlike flavor, semi-firm, rubbery, deep creamy yellow

EMMENTHALER
firm, flavorful Swiss cheese with holes, cream color

FETA
goat cheese, piquant, semi-soft, white

GORGONZOLA
tangy, piquant, medium soft, crumbly, straw color
streaked with blue veins

GOUDA
similar to Edam but smaller, mellow, semi-firm, rubbery, yellow-orange

GRUYÈRE
nutlike flavor, Swiss family, firm, smooth, creamy
yellow

JARLESBERG
sweet nutlike flavor, yellow

LIEDERKRANZ
tangy, soft and smooth, creamy yellow

LIMBURGER
pungent, strong flavor and odor, soft, creamy white

MONTEREY JACK
mild, semi-soft, hard when aged, yellow

MOZZARELLA
mild, semi-firm, rubbery, creamy white

MUENSTER
mild, mellow, semi-soft, straw color

NEUFCHÀTEL
resembles cream cheese, mild, soft, smooth, white

PARMESAN
pungent distinctive flavor, hard, straw color

PONT L'ÉVÊQUE
pungent, semi-soft, yellowish white

PORT DU SALUT
mellow to pungent, semi-soft and rubbery, creamy white

PROVOLONE
semi-sharp to sharp, firm and smooth, cream color

RACLETTE
mild, firm, creamy, tangy when melted, yellow

RICOTTA
mild, nutlike, semi-soft, white

ROMANO
sharp, hard, granular, yellowish white

ROQUEFORT
tangy, piquant, soft and crumbly, hard when dry, white with blue veins

STILTON
piquant, flaky, creamy white with blue veins

SWISS
mild, sweet, firm, elastic, large holes throughout, cream color

TILSIT
mellow, semi-firm, pale creamy yellow

TRAPPIST
mellow, semi-firm, yellow

index